Biting Back

About the Author

Claudia Cunningham has used her uniquely powerful combination of 12-step principles and vampire lore to empower others for nearly a decade. Her "Ask the Slayer" column was a regular feature in Women's Online Magazine and she continues to write a popular blog at practicalslayer.blogspot.com. Throughout her life, Claudia has both hosted and slain her fair share of bloodthirsty vampires. Now a vigilant Watcher, she avidly shares the power of love, community, and living in the light. A native of Milwaukee, and transplant from hither and yon, she lives in Montana with her handsome husband, Robert, and their trapeze-swinging daughter, Madeline Jane.

To Write to the Author

If you wish to contact the author or would like more information about this book, please write to the author in care of Llewellyn Worldwide and we will forward your request. Both the author and publisher appreciate hearing from you and learning of your enjoyment of this book and how it has helped you. Llewellyn Worldwide cannot guarantee that every letter written to the author can be answered, but all will be forwarded. Please write to:

Claudia Cunningham
c/o Llewellyn Worldwide
2143 Wooddale Drive
Woodbury, MN 55125-2989

Please enclose a self-addressed stamped envelope for reply, or $1.00 to cover costs. If outside the U.S.A., enclose an international postal reply coupon.

Many of Llewellyn's authors have websites with additional information and resources. For more information, please visit our website at

www.llewellyn.com

Biting Back

A No-Nonsense, {*No-Garlic*} Guide

TO FACING THE

Personal Vampires IN YOUR LIFE

CLAUDIA CUNNINGHAM

Llewellyn Publications
Woodbury, Minnesota

First Edition
First Printing, 2010

Cover design by Ellen Dahl
Editing by Laura Graves

Library of Congress Cataloging-in-Publication Data
Cunningham, Claudia, 1958–
Biting back: a no-nonsense, no-garlic guide to facing the personal vampires in your life / Claudia Cunningham.—1st ed.
p. cm.
ISBN 978-0-7387-1541-4
1. Vampires. I. Title.
GR830.V3C86 2010
398'.45—dc22

2010020283

Llewellyn Publications
A Division of Llewellyn Worldwide Ltd.
2143 Wooddale Drive
Woodbury, MN 55125-2989
www.llewellyn.com

Printed in the United States of America

Or,
How to Whittle the Stake that Works, Whether or Not We Choose to Use It

To my husband Robert and daughter Madeline Jane:
For keeps

Contents

II

Biting Back

III

Living in the Light

"Ask the Slayer" Columns

Ask the Slayer

WHAT *IS* THIS?

Dear Practical Vampire Slayer,

Not to offend you or anything, but ... is this for real? A manual for slaying vampires? Aren't you addressing a, well ... sort of specialized *audience?*

Sincerely,
Puzzled in St. Louis

Dear Puzzled,

No offense taken—and to answer your question: I think it all depends on how you define the word "vampire."

If what you're talking about are sharp fangs, pale skin, and silly accents, then you're probably referring to mythological vampires like Dracula, for instance.

But if what you're talking about are never-ending resentments, stolen property, lost time, and that creepy feeling you keep on getting that someone or something else besides you is running your life, then you're probably referring to *practical* vampires, which are, incidentally, the kind we'll be learning how to slay here.

Fortunately for us, both are evicted from our lives in the same way: with clear and precise revocations, and *always* in the light.

Yours,

PVS

The Practical Vampire Slayer

....

How to Use This Book

THERE IS A RULE IN VAMPIRE MYTHOLOGY which states that a vampire can't just walk into your house and start sucking your blood. *First,"* it says, *"the vampire must be invited."*

This rule usually shows up at some point in vampire books and movies, almost always mentioned in passing. You find it tucked into one scene or another, without further ado, as if it weren't the most intriguing aspect in any relationship between a vampire and its victim, or as if it were moderately interesting vampire triviæ someone thought would be cool to throw in the script.

Which it is not.

The invitation principle is not only one of the most provocative elements of vampire lore, but it is also the foundation of what I call "practical vampire slaying"—a method of blending vampire mythology with well-known spiritual principles designed to help us identify our real-life vampires and to make clear and informed decisions about whether we want to continue our relationships with them or not—decisions that some of us never even knew we had the power to make.

But I said I was going to tell you about how to use this book, so let's take care of that first.

It begins with a short self-test on whether or not you may be hosting vampires. After that, the book is divided into three sections.

In **Part I: From Darkness into Light**, we'll be talking about the problem of unhealthy relationships (i.e. "practical vampires") in our lives, and about the vocabulary, origins, and rules of practical vampire slaying. This section also contains examples of these practical vampires and descriptions of our relationships with them in more detail. We'll talk about the nature of vampires, the darkness in which they're born and thrive, and about the tricks they play in order to get the invitations they *must* have before they can enter our lives. Then, since taking responsibility for who we are and the choices we make is fundamental to practical vampire slaying, we'll also be looking at the nature of *ourselves*: the gifts of life and free will we've been granted, and we'll reflect on why in the world any of us would consider surrendering these precious gifts to a vampire in the first place. Oh, and something important: *You'll need a notebook, one you like to write in, and a pen you're comfortable using.* There are some important questions you'll be asking yourself as we go along, and seeing your answers in black and white will be vital to getting all you can out of the process.

Also, because we'll be discussing the gifts of life and free will, and because we'll be discussing the use of power, I ask that you *bring along your very own conception of a Higher Power, or God.* What that is to you personally is of no interest to me and has no bearing at all on your success or failure as vampire slayers—your God is *your* business. What *is* important to your success is that you bring that conception with you—however vague it might be—because you're going to need it. Real problems require real power to solve, and since nearly all of our work is (like practically everything else in life) of a spiritual nature, this is one source of power you're going to want to have ... or, if necessary, acquire as you go along. You never know what you'll see when you start to look inside—all of us are just *filled* with surprises.

In **Part II: Biting Back**, we'll be moving on to the solution, which we'll know by this time has much more to do with changing *ourselves* than it does with changing our vampires. There are specific instructions to follow, lists to make, and options to consider as we bring light to our relationships and the way we've behaved in them. We'll talk more about power and where to look for it, and finally, after we've done a few exercises, we'll learn exactly what our choices are for getting rid of our vampires, and how to execute each one of them.

Part III: Living in the Light, is about maintenance. Once you've got the hang of the slaying business, you'll want to know how to stay free of your vampires and to avoid future entanglements with them. This part convers some tips about how to keep yourself vampire-free and includes a section on "spiritual garlic"—an inner cleansing practice of self-evaluation used at the end of each day that helps you to stay current with yourself and "in the present," as they say. We'll talk about attitudes, and I'm going to tell you one of the best stories I've ever heard about God anywhere—one that has to do with gratitude—and then we'll be finished.

Or maybe I should say, "And then we'll have just begun."

Thanks for joining me.

Claudia Cunningham
The Practical Vampire Slayer

P.S. By the way, every now and then in the book, you'll come across a page that contains a "Dear Abby"–type column called "*Ask the Slayer*." These are just what they appear to be: letters from readers of my blog who wrote with questions about their vampires. My readers ask such perfect questions sometimes that I just had to include a few here; they have a special way of getting right to the heart of the vampire.

Self-Test

See? You need that notebook already.

Am I Hosting a Vampire?

True/False

1. Some people give me the creeps, but I'm always polite to them—even when their behavior toward me is repeatedly inappropriate or intimidating.

    ❑ True ❑ False

2. I freeze just for a second when the phone rings or there's a knock on my door.

    ❑ True ❑ False

3. I attract crazy people. Somehow, they always seem to find me.

    ❑ True ❑ False

4. There are times when I could swear I'm invisible: especially when I'm cooking and cleaning for people who seem to take it for granted.

    ❑ True ❑ False

5. I live with someone who says mean things about me, but I know they don't mean it. People just don't understand him/her the way I do.

    ❑ True ❑ False

6. Every morning on my way to work, I think about that jerk at the office and imagine *exactly* how I'm going to tell him off today.

    ❑ True ❑ False

7. I never know when certain people or neighbors are going to pop over, but I want folks to know that if they need someone to talk to, I'm always here for them.

    ❑ True ❑ False

8. I don't see the point in worrying about my appearance or fussing over makeup and nice clothes—I'm not that vain, and besides, who has the time?

    ❑ True ❑ False

9. I avoid a lot of deep-thinking and self-reflection. All that "new age" kind of thing just isn't my style.

    ❑ True ❑ False

10. I wish that somebody, just once, would say *thank you* to me.

    ❑ True ❑ False

Answer Key

1. If you answered "True" here, then you're playing a dangerous game: Vampires love to test our boundaries—or, as we like to refer to them around here, our "thresholds." Each time we allow people to treat us in a disrespectful or intimidating manner, we are inviting them to become vampires to us. (See chapter one, rule #1, regarding invitations.)
2. Everyday fears are some of the best diagnostic tools we have for determining whether or not we have a vampire in our lives. If you answered "True" to this one, there's a reason for it, and finding what that reason is and how to stop it is what practical vampire slaying is all about.
3. If you've noticed that you attract crazies but don't know why, this book will help you figure that out. If you answered "True" to this one, I'm here to tell you: attracting lunatics is not your "destiny." You have a choice. And freedom to choose is another thing practical vampire slaying is all about.
4. Vampires aren't the only ones who can't see their own reflections in the mirror. The sad fact is that as the vampire drains the host, the host's image will start to fade, too. If you answered "True" to this one and feel invisible sometimes, it could mean you're hosting a vampire.
5. Nice people who host vampires often feel they're the only ones who understand their vampires. If you answered "True" to this, you may not understand your partner as well as you think you do.
6. Vampires often come in the shape of resentments: of anger we feel not once about a particular person or

situation, but repeatedly. If this is true for you and you're experiencing the same anger about a certain person or situation again and again, you might have a vampire on your neck.

7. People who host vampires often feel an over-developed sense of responsibility about making their time and homes available to people who are only too happy to turn their problems (especially ones that never get solved) over to their hosts. If your answer was "true" here, you may be more than just a nice person. You may be hosting a vampire.
8. People who host vampires often perceive their own needs and self-care as unimportant, especially since they are so focused on the needs of others, others who often prove to be vampires. If you aren't the type that takes self-care seriously, you might be susceptible to vampire hosting.
9. If vampire hosts take time to analyze anyone, it's usually their vampires. They may complain or speculate about their vampires, but almost never consider the role they themselves play in the relationships they share. If you answered "True" to this one and don't like the idea of self-reflection, you're focusing just where your vampires want you to focus: on them and never yourself. And this *could* mean you're in what's known as the vampire's thrall. (See chapter one on the subject of thralls.)
10. If you answered "True" and you're feeling unappreciated, it's probably because you *are*. But we can change that. Practical vampire slaying is all about change and it's about gratitude, too.

    Is it ever.

"Vampires do exist."

—Dr. Abraham Van Helsing,
Dracula, by Bram Stoker

I

From Darkness into Light

1

The Fundamentals of Slaying

The Origin, the Vampire, the Vocabulary, and the Rules

A vampire can't just walk into your house and start sucking your blood. First, it has to be invited.

BACK IN THE DAY AND WHAT WITH one thing or another, it's probably safe to say I spent about half my time under the influence of drugs or alcohol, and the other half of it waiting to be under the influence of drugs or alcohol again. Those hours of waiting were hard: between the physical pain of abstinence and the emotional confusion that comes with the disease of addiction, they were as good as torture, and I was always looking for something to divert my attention from my misery—something that would help those long hours of sickness to pass.

Television and radio weren't strong enough to do the trick, but I found that reading, especially the novels of Stephen King, was fairly helpful. There was one book in particular that was about vampires, *'Salem's Lot*, and that's where I first heard about this rule that you have to invite a vampire in before it can suck your blood. *'Salem's Lot* is one of King's earliest books, and it's the story of a Master Vampire named Barlow who wants to make the little town of Jerusalem's Lot his own, only first he's going to have to fight a group of slayers who assemble there to stop him. I've read that book more times than I care to admit, but this rule about invitations has impressed me every time.

Years later, when I was finally ready to stop drinking, I came across this invitation rule again—only this time it wasn't in a book about vampires, it was in a program of recovery. One of the first things I learned when I got there was that if I wanted to be sane and sober, I was going to have to change the way I looked at my life and its problems. I learned that if I wanted to live happily, I was going to have to start asking myself, each time I found myself in a mess, exactly what I had contributed to the creation of that mess. That's right, you heard me: even though it was obvious to everyone I was having a terrible time and never ever would have chosen to be in such misery, I was still expected to take some responsibility for how the misery had come into my life—almost as if I'd invited it in myself!

And I just knew I'd heard that somewhere before.

Combining the spiritual principles I've learned as a member of a 12-step group with my love of vampire mythology has helped me create a method for solving the kinds of problems that so many of us have with draining and unhealthy relationships—a method I call "practical vampire slaying."

Practical vampires are the kind we deal with every day; they are the very real and influential people, institutions, and beliefs that shape our lives and how we live them, only they prefer to exert their influence from in the dark, which is where they live. When I got into recovery and learned about the power of bringing light to the parts of myself I'd been trying so hard to keep in the dark, and began to discover, too, the freedom that comes with taking responsibility for the people and things that enter my life, I saw there was much more to this correlation between vampire slaying and spiritual recovery than just the invitation rule alone. I saw these parallels in every vampire book, movie, and television show I came across—just sitting there, waiting for someone to come along and notice them.

The Vampire

Practical vampires like to give the impression of being an unchangeable part of our lives, but they're really not. We may think their presence is somehow natural or inevitable, but making us believe that is just part of the vampire's game, and their status in our lives is by no means fixed. As the principles of vampire slaying will show: if we have the power to invite them into our lives, then we also have the power to throw them out. These are our lives we're talking about here, and our choices to make about how we want to live them.

For some of us the vampire comes in the shape of a spouse, child, friend, or employer who minimizes or refuses to acknowledge all we do for them. These people feed on taking us for granted, and leave us more frustrated and hurt than we sometimes think we can stand.

For others, it's an ex-girlfriend who still hasn't gotten around to moving out or an ex-boyfriend who just cannot understand that breaking up means, "stop calling me, stop writing me, and while you're at it—stop stalking me, too." These types obviously need more comprehensive definitions of the words "finished," "over with," and "done"—which, by the way, we can give them.

Many of us are hosting vampires that enter our lives as addictions: some to alcohol or drugs, some to shopping or gambling, some to exercise or starvation—you name it—and the secrets they force us to keep about ourselves are pushing us into the dark and draining the soul out of us so fast we hardly know what bit us.

Then too, there are the vampires we've never even met: the telemarketers and junk-mailers, the credit card companies and banks, the people in front of us who drive like sightseers any time we're in a rush to get somewhere, and even television news analysts who don't know the difference between having a personality and having a personality disorder; all of these can feed on our good will and dispositions, becoming vampires to us in a matter of moments. Where was the happiness and love we had to share with others only a minute ago? After lending the last of our patience to these irritations? Gone. Just like that.

But confidentially, it's not just those vampires on the *outside*, is it? Some of the noisiest, meanest-talking vampires live right inside our own minds. They hardly ever let us eat a meal in peace, they're so busy calculating calorie and fat content. They warn us not in join in the volleyball game because we're too clumsy and we'll look foolish if we try. They keep us from dressing the way we want because we need to be a smaller size before we're allowed to buy clothes we actually like. They advise us not to risk expressing an opinion or the way we feel because we're sure to sound ridiculous. They love to hide and chatter on about us in the dark where we can't see them, but still have to listen to every word they say.

These are vampires in the monstrous sense of the word, and when it comes to dealing with them, there's one thing to remember: no matter what shape they take or how big or small they might be, not one of them got into our lives without our say-so, our permission, or our invitation. Those are the rules.

Our Vocabulary

Vampire mythology has a vocabulary all its own, so before we go any further, I'd like to define a few terms we'll be using.

Invitations

The invitations we extend to our vampires are really no different from the invitations we extend to other people and things every day: we invite them into our lives, and in so doing, become their hosts. They serve in the same way any other invitation does. Except where our practical vampires are concerned, when it comes to the invitations we extend to them, we almost never realize exactly what we've invited in until *after* they've crossed our thresholds.

When we failed to ask that telemarketer to simply "take us off the list," we thought we were just letting some poor guy make his pitch. We had five minutes to give him—sure—but we had no idea we were inviting not only him but also his company and all their relatives in for endless future calls and solicitations.

When we told our employer that we'd be happy to work late that first time and assumed (as normal people do) that it was a one-time-emergency-only thing: we never dreamed we were inviting late night work in for the rest of our time on that job or that our boss would expect all future overtime and night work to go unquestioned.

Or when we took the time to listen to that woman-we-hardly-knew's woes in the grocery store that time: we thought she'd appreciate our kindness and maybe even apologize the next time we saw her for unloading on us that way. But she seems instead to have adopted us as her personal counselor, and we've become like a paratrooper in our own town, ducking and running to avoid her nearly everywhere we go.

The thing about vampires is that we never know how much hosting we've really signed up for. Until we do, that is.

Hosts

Hosts are all the great people that practical vampires feed on—by which I mean you, me, and anyone else who's invited them in. Simply stated: when you've got a vampire clamped to your neck, that makes you the host of that vampire. It doesn't matter what your sex or creed is, whom you voted for, how many courses in psychology you've taken, or what color underwear you wear: if you don't know how to spot a vampire or what turns your hosting switch to "on," you're just as likely to wind up with a vampire on your neck as the next guy. It's surprising how many people think they're exempt, and how many think that just because they can see the vampire coming, they are therefore somehow qualified to avoid it. Unfortunately for them, that's not how it works, and since our motto here is "Host, know thyself," that's where we aim our searchlights: not at our vampires, but at *ourselves*. Remember what I said about power? If we don't stop looking at our vampires and start focusing on how we extend our invitations to them instead, we're going to be sunk without power when the time finally comes that we want to revoke those invitations.

Thresholds

The best way to think about thresholds as they relate to practical vampire slaying is to picture the doorway or threshold of your home. It represents the boundary between all you allow to come inside and all that remains outside, right? Just as you are the owner of your home and host to all that comes over its threshold, so you are the owner of your life and host to all that comes over its threshold, too. Thus, a vampire must receive your invitation before it can cross the threshold into your life.

The trick with thresholds is figuring out exactly where they are. Identifying where the thresholds in our homes are is a pretty simple thing, but identifying thresholds in our lives can be a delicate matter. Determining where our personal thresholds lie is in fact one of the most challenging aspects of practical vampire slaying, and one we'll need to learn well if we want to survive.

Solicitations

When a vampire asks to be invited in, it is what's known as a "solicitation." It sounds crazy, I know, but if we don't invite them over our thresholds quick enough they'll find a way to squeeze an invitation out of us so that we do. It's not like they're straightforward or honest about it—though don't get me wrong, most of the time they're so devious we can't even remember how they got from outside to in. But it happens, and they're good at it, which they have to be, after all. If you had an insatiable appetite, you'd get pretty good at ordering your meals, too.

Revocations

Once we realize and acknowledge responsibility for extending an invitation, we then have the authority to revoke or withdraw it, and that's what a revocation is: it gives official notice to our vampires that they are no longer welcome in our "homes" and that their invitations to be there have been withdrawn. Here's an excellent example of the kind of revocation that works:

"Get out of here! I revoke my invitation!"

It's clear, yes? And as you can see, the host extends the invitation/the host revokes the invitation. Extend/Revoke. Extend/Revoke. Both are our prerogative and our responsibility.

The Thrall

Have you ever noticed how victims in vampire movies always fall into a dopey, trancelike state whenever their vampires are around? Well, that's how they dramatize the "thrall" in Hollywood, but in real life, the thrall of our practical vampires is much more. Theirs is actually a highly persuasive, hypnotic power they exert that makes us strangely susceptible to their suggestions, no matter how demanding or ridiculous those suggestions might be.

My friend Angela, for instance, had a vampire show up at her house unexpectedly one day to ask if she'd like to go with him to a party. He gave her no warning, and the party had already begun—which, by the way, is just so typical: vampires just love to solicit their invitations in the form of last-minute plans and emergencies. But since she'd lost quite a bit of blood (metaphorically speaking) the last time they'd been together, and since her wounds were still, so to speak, fresh on her neck, she was able to turn him down. What she couldn't understand after he'd left, though, was why she'd even been *considering* his proposition.

"The weird thing is that I was actually thinking about going with him!" she laughed, "and I just can't believe I would even consider it, especially when I'm still trying to recover from the last time I saw him!"

Angela's story illustrates so perfectly how we fall under their spell. All her vampire had to do was show up at her place without warning, make eye contact with her, and presto—there she was, in his thrall and vulnerable to his suggestions, no matter how absurd those suggestions would seem to her only moments after he'd left.

The vampires' thrall—keep it in mind. I have to tell you, this is one thing I hear from slayers all the time. They're always calling to tell me how, once they understood what the thrall was, it ceased to have any power over them. As soon as they knew what their vampire was up to—poof!—its power to manipulate them was gone.

Vampire: 0, Host: 1. Just what we're shooting for.

Practical Vampire Slayers

This group includes you, me, our best friends, that guy at the bus stop, and any other host who expresses a desire to solve their vampire problems, who studies and practices the vampire rules, and who chooses to take responsibility for their lives so they can make informed, clear, and above all, *free* choices about how they want to live them. Maybe they'll slay their vampires and maybe they won't, but if they practice the principles outlined in this book, they'll always have the freedom to choose *and* the stake that works—just in case they decide they ever want to use it.

Watchers

For every vampire slayer or group of vampire slayers, there is a mentor or advisor—someone who knows all there is to know about vampires and vampire slaying. Their job is teach, advise, and support the slayer.

If you're acquainted with vampire literature or movies, you've already seen your share of Watchers whether you know it or not: In *Dracula,* the Watcher is Dr. Abraham Van Helsing, who has a tendency toward... long-windedness, and as a result, winds up doing a heck of a lot more slayer-advising than he does actual vampire-slaying.

In *Buffy the Vampire Slayer*, there is a character named Rupert Giles, who acts as Buffy's advisor and trainer. He is the first of his kind I ever heard refer to himself as "Watcher," and I *think* I might be stealing this term from him.

Matt Burke in Stephen King's *'Salem's Lot* is a teacher-turned-Watcher who counsels the little group of slayers in that story. He's my favorite by far, because even though he was scared, he stepped up to do the job when he was needed. He studied as much as he could find about vampire slaying as fast as possible, and then shared all he'd learned with his friends so they might save the town they loved. That makes him the definitive Watcher to me, since he did what all the finest Watchers do: which is simply the best they can, and always in the name of love.

Most of us who choose to slay our vampires will almost certainly become Watchers one day ourselves—not only because the best way to hold on to all we've learned is by giving it away, but also because that's just the way these things work, and giving it away is something we'll just really want to do.

It's time to take our definitions and move on to the next step, which is to review the list of vampire rules I promised you. These are the rules from mythology that govern our real-life slaying, and as you might have guessed by now, they're not made for breaking.

The Rules

Rule #1: Vampires can't just walk into your house and start sucking your blood. First, they have to be invited.

Forget about dodging the blame, pointing the finger, making excuses, or saying it's "their fault." If we've got a vampire in our lives, it's because we invited it in. This isn't meant to suggest in any way that we're looking for trouble when we extend our invitations. This rule's only function is to remind us that we were there when our vampires came knocking and that, in one way or another, we also let them in.

Rule #2: Vampires do not need an invitation every time they cross the threshold. One invitation grants a lifetime pass.

Yes. It's horrid, I know, but it is the rule. And it certainly goes a long way toward explaining why some people think they have the right to come and go in our lives whenever they please—to say nothing of why so many of them never leave at all.

Rule #3: Every host has the option to revoke an invitation they've extended to a vampire, but they have to know the rules if they want to do it right.

That's what we'll be learning here: the rules for revoking our invitations and the rules for exercising a few other options, too. There's more than one way to skin a vampire, you know—and if we want to be truly free, we'll need to know every one of them. Freedom is the most wonderful thing, and because it always entails responsibility, it leads us naturally to:

Rule #4: Hosts must claim responsibility for their invitations before they can reclaim their power to revoke them.

In a roundabout way, this is our first lesson in power and it's also our first step in learning where to look for it from now on. Responsibility and power go hand-in-hand, and when we refuse to take responsibility for our invitations, we're giving up our power, too. From now on when we're searching for power we'll remember this rule about responsibility, and then go straight to our mirrors—where we'll have learned to find both.

Rule #5: Above all, our revocations must be clear. Before we can issue a revocation telling our vampires what we want, we have to know exactly what that is ourselves.

Revoking our invitations requires clarity: clarity about our vampires, our invitations, and most of all, ourselves. There's a lot more to revoking an invitation than simply telling a vampire to beat it. The steps we take to find that clarity about what we really want—prior to issuing our revocations—are what really count.

Rule #6: All vampires' appetites are insatiable.

"Insatiable appetites" are exactly what they sound like: the kind of appetites that can never be satisfied or go away. A vampire can no more be a "little" insatiable than a woman can be a "little" pregnant. Insatiability is an all or nothing deal, in spite of how few of us actually believe that when it comes to our own vampires. No matter how we try to tell ourselves that if we can just provide them with enough of what they want that they'll be satisified, it's never going to work. Insatiability is a definitive quality in vampires, practical or not, which means there's no getting around it—not ever.

Rule #7: Never look into a vampire's eyes.

This rule, like all the others, has an important metaphorical meaning as well as a literal one. Just as there is more than one way define a vampire, there is also more than one way to define "looking into a vampire's eyes." Think metaphorically, and you'll see what I mean.

Let's say, for instance, you've got a vampire friend who's complained to you about the same marital problems she's been having, *ad infinitum*, for more than five years now. Engaging in this conversation with her again and again, metaphorically speaking, is just the same as locking eyes with a vampire. In fact, looking into a vampire's eyes can be a lot like extending an invitation, and the more we practice looking at ourselves instead, the clearer those invitations we're extending will become to us. Practice makes perfect—or at the very least makes progress, which is another thing we're shooting for around here.

Rule #8: A vampire cannot see its own reflection in a mirror.

Vampire mythology tells us this is true, and so does real life. I've never known a practical vampire yet who has the slightest idea about the hurt they cause or even the tiniest bit of interest in looking in the mirror and examining who they really are. Self-searching usually leads to enlightenment, and I'm sure I don't have to tell you how little light of any kind our vampires want in their lives.

There will be more rules for us to learn as we go along, and this is as far as we need to go for now. There is one more thing I want you to keep in mind: vampires can be very tricky, and have an amazing talent for causing the most inexplicable amnesia in us. That's one reason we'll be talking later on about the importance of creating a community for ourselves. Community provides a great source of power; it keeps us safe and in the light, and we need it to keep reminding each other about those rules we're sure to forget.

We're ready to begin. As I said, we'll be learning more about our vampires and the rules that govern them, but in the end I expect we'll be learning most about ourselves. As practical vampire slayers, we know the change we want in our lives begins with us—not with our vampires. Trying to change the vampire? That's not what we're doing here, and that's exactly why this rule about their needing our invitations is so important: it serves as a gentle tap on the shoulder, reminding us that if we really want to be free of our vampires, we'd better quit paying so much attention to them, and start paying more attention to ourselves instead.

There's just one more rule I want to tell you about. It seems almost too obvious to mention, but I think I'd better, since people seem to have the hardest time remembering it. I'm speaking of the consequences that people who never get around to revoking their invitations have to pay—you know, those folks who think they're different and the rules don't apply to them, so they let their vampires feed and feed.

Do you remember what happens to all those nice people—the ones who are too busy to revoke their invitations?

Rule #9: When it comes to hosts who never revoke their invitations:

They become vampires too.

Ask the Slayer

Not Goth

Dear PVS,

I'm 19 years old, and not Goth. I am fairly normal by most standards, but three female vampires have tried to start relationships with me in the past month.

Am I attracting this or do I just have really bad luck?

Sincerely,
Bob

Dear Bob,

First off, you don't need to be Goth to attract a vampire, and the vampires we're talking about here aren't overly impressed with image—what turns them on is vulnerability and a potentially good meal. What they want is a way to get in and lots to eat once they've crossed the threshold. Think "invitations." Think "insatiable appetites."

Practical vampires are not people playing dress-up or members of any particular community. Practical vampires are defined not by what they do but rather by how they affect us. It can be pretty hard to tell until after we've invited them over our thresholds. After that, and in one way or another, we're sure to learn whether they're the biting type or not.

That's what life is all about, though: having the free will to invite whatever we like into our lives. The responsible thing to do is to learn how to revoke your invitation—just in case it turns out to be one of these hungry predators that you've invited. Then you'll have the freedom to extend your invitations as you please, because you'll know what to do when one of them turns out to be a biter.

Best of luck, Bob.

PVS

....

2

When a Vampire Calls

How They Solicit Their Invitations

THERE ARE PLENTY OF ADVANTAGES TO APPLYING the invitation rule to our lives, but one I especially like is how it can help ease that feeling of helplessness we get sometimes—you know, that sense we get that so much of what happens to us is completely out of our control. The list of things we can't control is, after all, a fairly long one. There are the obvious things like the weather, gravity, and mortality, but then there are the more subtle things we're more apt to forget—like the fact that we have no control over the way other people see things, behave, and feel. The fact is, most things in life fall under the heading of "stuff we don't get to be the boss of." But that's what makes this rule about having to invite our vampires in so consoling. At least we know now that when we discover it's a vampire that's crossed the threshold into our lives, we'll have the comfort of knowing we can get them back to the other side of the line again, any time we want. The vampire rules might seem daunting in terms of the responsibility we'll be learning to take for ourselves, but on the flip side, they also remind us that there are some things in life we *can* control.

The trouble with vampires, though, is that even when we know we've played a part in how they got into our lives, it's still not always so easy to see where we invited them in, or to get over the sneaking suspicion that—in one way or another—we were tricked into extending our invitations.

Vampire Solicitations

We're right to be suspicious. Practical vampires, just like their mythological counterparts, are acutely aware of the rules about power. They know that the moment we see and claim responsibility for our invitations will also be the moment we claim our power to revoke them, so it's in their best interests to keep us as unconscious and in the dark about our invitations to them as they possibly can. Some of our vampires' solicitations are deliberately misleading and some—as we'll see a little later—are not. But since you'll want to be able to recognize them either way, what follows here is a list of some of the most common strategies our vampires use in their solicitations.

Let's start with a few of their most intentionally deceitful.

Bait and Switch

I'd been living in Alaska for about a year when I went to visit my sister Julia in Chicago. We were headed up Dearborn Street on foot one morning and a man approached me, asking for a match. I stopped, dug into my coat pocket (I was a smoker at the time) and produced the matchbook. As I handed it over, he moved a little closer to me and said, "Do you have a cigarette?"

I scowled disapprovingly, but reached into my pocket again. When I gave him the cigarette, he asked me for a quarter. I laughed, obviously irritated, and started for my pocket again, but Julia, having seen all she could stand, grabbed my arm and urged me to resume walking.

She said, "Did you make eye contact with him?" Like there was something wrong with eye contact.

"Yes," I said, "I *look* at people."

"Well," she said, "that's how he picked you out—how he knew you'd make a good target. All that jazz about matches and cigarettes was just to see how close you'd let him get. When he got close enough, he was going to grab your purse." She looked at me. "He was getting pretty close," she said.

She was right, naturally. Looking back on it, I can now see what a huge red flag it was that this guy needed *my* matches, you know? *Just* mine. He didn't need matches from the middle-aged and male native Chicagoan who'd passed him ahead; he needed them from the young and female out-of-towner who made eye contact with him—me, of course. Typical prey. Typical vampire.

The whole incident reminds me of the interaction between Dracula and his prey in a scene from the movie *Bram Stoker's Dracula*—the one where he first solicits his invitation from the story's heroine, Mina Harker. If you haven't seen this movie, you should: parts of it illustrate so well the rules we're talking about here, and this scene in particular is one of my favorites.

The year is around 1900, and as the scene opens we witness a young Dracula (charismatically played by Gary Oldman) cruising the streets of London. At first we're not sure what he's up to, but when we see the beautiful Miss Mina (played sweetly by Winona Ryder) on the opposite side of the street, we understand that he's out hunting, and that she's the prey.

He stops walking and stares at her as she moves down the street. When she fails to return his gaze, he says quietly,

"See me. See me now."

Slowly she turns her head and makes—what else—*eye contact* with him, and then walks into a store. Dracula crosses the street, and as she's leaving the store he bumps into her, causing a package to drop from her hand—which he neatly rescues and then quickly uses as a pretext to *determine her threshold* and *solicit his invitation*. Remember how that Chicago vampire tried to do that with me?

Matches, cigarettes, rescued packages, whatever.

He launches into his solicitation by asking her for directions, because just like Mr. Windy City, he apparently needs only her directions, and not some other pedestrian's. She's not falling for it, though, and she curtly suggests that if he needs help finding his way around, that he should probably "go buy a map."

What's so surprising though, is Dracula's reaction to her dismissal, because he appears to be absolutely fine with it . . . and for a moment, we have to wonder at his indifference. But then we get it: for predators like these, whether they ever get the matches or directions they're asking for is far from the point. What they're seeking is *engagement*. What does Dracula care if Miss Mina won't give him directions? He just wants to keep the interaction going, the ball in play. Engagement is what he's after.

And Miss Mina *is* engaged. Like me with the guy on Dearborn Street, she's a bit stiff, but she's still responding, still interacting. She's told him to "go buy a map," but hasn't specifically told him to "go away and don't come back." She feels she's implied that, and that anyone with just the tiniest grain of sense should be able to take the hint.

This is a common mistake. In our efforts to preserve decorum, we, like Miss Mina, often fail to tell vampires what's really on our minds—like the fact that we want them to leave, for instance—and instead wait desperately for them to "take the hint."

Which brings us to the fantastically important:

Rule # 10: Vampires don't take hints. It's their special gift. They are immune to innuendo.

And what a handy immunity it is for them, too, especially since so many of us find it nearly impossible to tell them (point-blank) to just get lost. What is this aversion we have to speaking clearly and directly about what we want, anyway? Are we afraid that by being honest with them we'll hurt their feelings? Or are we afraid we'll have to admit to ourselves that we're not quite as nice as we like to think we are? Do we imagine that they'll get mad and start yelling at us? Whatever our reasons, our vampires must be familiar with them, because they sure seem to know which buttons to push and when to push them. How broad their inward smiles must be as they observe our struggles to find an indirect way of saying "no" to them—one they know they'll be immune to no matter how carefully we phrase it. How they must savor those moments—watching us hesitate and stammer, trying so hard to find a way of both saying and not saying what we mean at the same time. And how tremendously liberating it would be for us if we'd just stop dropping all these ludicrously vague *hints*, and start being clear with them, instead.

But no, people almost always insist on handling vampires "their own way" and that includes Miss Mina, unfortunately for her.

Dracula approaches her once more, but this time she's so abrupt with him that he actually apologizes for bothering her and starts to walk away... but she calls him back. Let me say that again: *She calls him back*. Guess what for? To apologize! She wants to tell him she's sorry for being so rude! Isn't that great? He keeps bugging her until her hints get nasty, and then she ends up feeling she owes him an apology.

The next thing you know he's waltzing her into a theatre where pornographic movies are being shown, and quicker than you can say, "I didn't even think vampires were real," he's lured her into a private room and his fangs are out.

But that's how it goes: one minute you're trying not to be a prude, and the next you're being initiated into the ranks of the undead.

Shameless Lies

Many of our vampires' solicitations come in the form of outright lies—lies designed to suggest we have much to gain by inviting them in. Vampires aren't known for their high moral standards, and they're not above trying to make it sound like there's going to be something really cool in it for *us* if we allow them to cross our thresholds.

Telemarketers employ this type of solicitation every day. They're always calling to give us some once-in-a-lifetime, about-to-expire-at-any-second offer if only we'll provide them with a minute of our time. That's precisely what they ask us for, too:

> *Hi, Mr. Fill-in-Your-Name! I'd like to tell you about a no-risk way to make extra income for you and your loved ones, if I can just get a minute of your time.*

Mm-hmm. But these guys aren't out to win awards for honesty and fair play; they're just trying to get in. Just as the average vampire won't be warning us that they want to suck our blood, so the average telemarketer won't be warning us that they've called to see how much of our money or personal information they can weasel out of us. Vampires rarely get their meals by telling us the truth about how hungry they are or what they want to eat.

It can be a hard thing to detect, though, especially if we're honest people who aren't in the habit of purposely misleading other people ourselves. However, misleading people is exactly what these guys get paid to do, and lying is just good business practice as far as they're concerned.

Their first priority is to get our invitations, and they're more than happy to use our own integrity against us in order to get them. They know honest people don't have enough experience with lying to know when they're being lied to themselves, and they'll use that virtue to get their invitations and cross our thresholds every chance they get.

Later, they'll feed.

Pointless Exercises

For years I have delighted in the practice certain credit card companies have of sending me applications that contain little stickers they want me to move from one page to another. Have you ever gotten those? They're colorful and shiny and usually have things like "PRE-APPROVED" and "*Please send to the Pre-Approval Department*" (the "Pre-Approval Department!" Right.) stamped all over them.

Beneath one of the stickers it usually says something like:

Claudia, use this sticker to request your new credit card!

"Wow," I think, "a shiny new sticker—and with my first name on it, too! It's almost like we're already ... *sniff* ... friends!"

Next I see they've enclosed yet another sheet of paper with a little colored square exactly the same size as my special sticker on it. Beneath it reads the text,

Claudia (me again!),
Remove sticker from envelope and place
here to expedite processing.

Then, in the spirit of helpfulness, they've drawn a huge red arrow pointing to the square where I'm to place the sticker.

It's an interesting proposal. "Just think," I tell myself, "if I can successfully navigate this sticker from one page to another, thereby *expediting processing* for my friends at Blahblahcard, I can look forward to years or perhaps even decades of relentless lying, trickery, intrusion, and debt."

Suck. Slurp. Smack.

I confess that until I studied the techniques perfected by that mugger in Chicago and even Dracula himself, I didn't really understand why credit card companies were so anxious to have us perform acrobatics like these, but I get it now.

They're taking measurements.

Just like that mugger, they're calculating how cooperative their prey is. And just like Dracula, they're untiring predators who begin their solicitations with engagement. In a stroke of marketing genius, they have devised a solicitation that not only engages their customer's participation, but measures their vulnerability to suggestion at the same time. I believe that any person willing to execute their instructions and deposit the whole sticky mess in the mail (thereby executing their invitation) graduates immediately to that company's *Special Donor List,* and is subsequently targeted for every bloodletting scam their corporate greed can devise.

Can you say, "insatiable appetites?"

Of course, the nice thing about solicitations by mail is that we don't have to deal with them if we don't want to. We can tear them up and throw them away.

But when it's our friends or family coming around, hungry and eyeballing us for a meal, it's not so easy just to tear *them* up and throw them in the garbage, is it? For one thing, they're coming to us live and in person: that makes them hard to avoid.

But for another, these are the people who know us best, and if they're vampires and family members both, they can often be almost impossible to escape.

Family or Not: The Vampire's Needs Always Come First

Let's face it: sometimes our own family members can be the worst vampires of all. I received an email from a woman who was having so much trouble with a vampire-sister of hers that she was getting ready to pack her bags and move to another state just to get away from her.

She began by explaining that she and her sister had been interacting with each other in a typical vampire/host manner for so long that both her invitations and her sister's feedings had become almost routine: a seemingly "normal" way of relating to each other that she felt powerless to stop.

What was frustrating her most, though, was a belief she had (and more to the point, that her vampire *knew* she had) that a simple refusal to her sister was insufficient; that she owed her vampire an explanation every time she told her "no." So if, for example, her sister said she needed help cleaning her house, raking her leaves, doing her shopping, or taking care of her kids, then she—the host—felt unable to answer, "I *don't want* to help you with that today." At some point this poor woman became allergic to the word *no* and for her it was an allergy that (and I mean this now) was going to kill her if she didn't do something about it pretty soon.

There are more ways to die than our hearts stopping on us, you know. There's *living death* too—a way of moving through our days that may seem like living, but it's not in service to ourselves. We live to serve "another," and I don't mean our Higher Power or God when I say that, either. I mean another person, thing, or belief that hurts us—a vampire that will drain us until we're either dead or become vampires ourselves. We don't call them "undead" for nothing, which is excellent reason to remember what happens to people who go on feeding their vampires indefinitely. You know what I mean.

And to say that these feedings could "kill" her is no exaggeration, since they're already stealing her life: she spends hours thinking up excuses to make and hints to drop for her vampire, and then spends even more time frustrated by the fact that none of those excuses or hints are working.

Talk about the definitive thrall! She's either feeding her vampire, dreading her vampire's next feeding, working on a way to avoid her vampire's next feeding, or beating her head against the wall because none of her plans to extricate herself are working. She has the same problem a lot of hosts have, which is imagining she can read her vampire's mind. She truly believes that if she can figure her vampire out, she'll be able to provide the magic excuse or hint that will remove her sister from her neck.

The trouble with vampires, though, is that they have a funny way of turning those excuses and hints into more solicitations. So if a host says, "Gosh, I'm too busy today to babysit. I only have an hour before I have to go to work," then the vampire will simply turn that inside-out and say, "Oh! Even an hour would be great! I'll drop the kids off in just a minute!"

Another fatal characteristic this woman shares with other classic hosts is the belief that if she can anticipate her vampire's next demand, she can supply it, and then, because her vampire's appetite will supposedly be satisfied, it will buy her a little freedom for a while. The host's strategy here might be to offer to babysit *before* her sister asks her to, so that her sister will (theoretically) then return the favor by giving her a break. This host, like so many, imagines that by anticipating her vampire's appetites and trying to satisfy them, she can appeal to her vampire's sense of proportion and fairness.

Do you want to laugh first, or should I just go ahead and start without you?

An "insatiable appetite" is just that: an unquenchable craving to consume that *has* no sense of proportion or normalcy—and what's killing many of us hosts is our refusal to believe that. We tell ourselves that if our vampires see how much we do for them and how well we do it, they'll surely consider it more than our fair share and stop asking us for more—especially when the vampire is a member of our own family and raised, supposedly, on the same standards and morals that we were. We tell ourselves they should know better and should behave better, too—only appetite, in this case, wins out over breeding. Kin or not, our vampires simply do not have the ability to see themselves or the truth about their appetites. Just as the fact that they *cannot see themselves* defines them as vampires, so the fact that we *can see* the truth about ourselves defines us as people with free will and the power to change. Thus, as practical vampire slayers, we must forget about trying to read their minds or satisfy their appetites (which we can never do), and instead pay attention to our own thinking and motives (which we certainly can).

While our own vampire scenarios or the degree to which we're enthralled by our vampires may be different from this woman's, the fear that lurks behind them and makes us slaves to our vampires' appetites is the same. Just like her, we are afraid to say that we *don't want* to help, that *our own needs are important*, that we have thresholds, and that no vampires—even family members—have our permission to cross them.

Of course, we have to know where our thresholds are before we can tell our vampires to stay on the other side of them, and we need to know what we want before we can be clear with anyone else about that, too. But those are both parts of the stake we'll be shaping for ourselves so we can be free of our vampires. Remember: there are times when our vampires secure their invitations without trickery or solicitations of any kind. Accidental invitations can happen and do every day.

The Accidental Vampire

Let's say you have a friend or relative who's been sleeping in your guest room—sans rent—for maybe the past six or seven months.

One morning you're hunting for the coffee creamer you *know* was still in the refrigerator when you went to bed the night before, and asking yourself how yon vampire, now digesting fond-remembered coffee creamer in the spare room, ever came to be there in the first place.

As you look back on it, the invitation *was* actually your idea: When you saw they were in trouble and needed a little help getting back on their feet, you practically insisted (extended an invitation) they stay with you. They certainly hadn't asked (solicited) to come in, but back then they were different (still among the living) somehow. They didn't seem so dependent and demanding (bloodthirsty and insatiable) in those days; and come to think of it, you didn't feel any actual suspicion or resentment (blood loss or anemia) for the first week or two they were there. Something changed, though, and before you knew it, they were moving their furniture and clothes (caskets and shrouds) in, and pretty soon after that they stopped even *pretending* they wanted to pay rent. They didn't seem particularly "undead" when you first invited them in, so what the heck happened here, anyway?

You may not be aware of this, but there can be a transition time for vampires. Sometimes we invite them in before they've completed their conversion to vampire-hood... ness... or undead status. I mean before they've *actually* become 100 percent vampire.

We see this illustrated in Bram Stoker's book *Dracula*, as poor Miss Mina struggles with Dracula's repeated visits to feed on her. At one point, she seems to be neither human nor vampire: faint, confused, nervous, and often sick. She exhibits all the classic symptoms we see in hosts whose vampires keep returning to feed, but haven't yet finished the job. It can get pretty gross, I know—watching people deteriorate as they make the transition from human to vampire. But it happens to people, and it can happen to *our* people—to our loved ones struggling with their own vampires: sadly and slowly but surely making the transition to Team Vampire themselves. When it comes to these guys, one minute we can trust that our coffee creamer is in the fridge, and the next minute almost anything we own can turn up missing. Remember, this all happened without their having even once solicited an invitation from us.

You know that rule about our vampires needing only one invitation to get in? This is a perfect example of that rule, because as you can see, even when we invite them in before they've made the transition and without their solicitation, that first invitation is still good and binding.

Those are the rules.

The Solicitation Turnaround

There is a favorite irregularity of mine to be found among the usual protocol of solicitations, and it's one that Dracula uses—again, in the classic by Bram Stoker. See if art imitates life for you as much as it does for me here.

It's early in the story, and Dracula is still in his homeland of Transylvania, hanging around the castle. We haven't seen him knocking on any victims' doors yet, but he has, interestingly enough, invited a potential victim to knock on his. It's a fascinating turn of solicitation when he gets the ambitious but sadly naïve real estate agent Jonathan Harker to come to the castle. And I believe it also presents a problem with vampire etiquette that some of us might not have anticipated.

Vampires are terrifically clever when it comes to dodging responsibility for their actions. Not only do they want to suck their host's blood, but they want to be sure they don't get blamed for it, too. Even more than the rest of us, they loathe the prospect of taking responsibility for their actions, which is the main reason, I've always thought, they insist upon receiving our invitations in the first place.

When our vampires secure their invitations before entering, it's not because their manners are so lovely or because they're just naturally polite: they do it because they want to be prepared. They have enough experience with this whole bloodsucking thing to know that one day the host is sure to start complaining, and when that day comes, the vampire will be ready.

"Listen, pal," they'll tell us, "This wasn't *my* idea! *You're* the one who invited *me* in, remember?" Of course that's not such an easy or even appropriate thing for a vampire to say when it's *the vampire* who invites *the victim in*. This transfer of responsibility can be a delicate thing for a vampire to handle gracefully—although one has to hand it to Dracula for finding such an elegant solution to the problem. When Mr. Harker comes to the castle door, he tells us Dracula opens up and says, "with strange intonation,"

"Welcome to my house. Enter freely and of your own will!"

I can't stop myself from smiling every time I read that, because Dracula is such a Master, you know? In that one simple statement he's completely absolved himself of any responsibility for what happens next in his relationship with Mr. Harker. He's made it clear that any decision Mr. Harker makes is of his own free will, and now it's up to him to either accept the Count's conditions for entry into the castle or to reject them. *Spoiler*: He accepts them—poor guy—and then things get, well ... pretty strange in his life for a while after that.

Had it been someone with knowledge of the vampire rules knocking on the Count's door, though—someone like ... oh, say, *me*, for instance—and he'd suggested, however smoothly, that I should "enter of my own free will," the scene might have played out a little differently.

I can see myself signaling the coachman to hold on for a second, and then nonchalantly turning to the Count and asking, "So what did you mean by that 'of my own free will' thing?"

And he'd probably have said something like, "Oh, nothing really. It's just a little custom I like to observe with some of my guests."

"Oh?"

"Oh yes, indeed ... and I thought if we could come to some sort of an understanding about your *will* in all of this ... I was thinking I might ask you to be a bit more specific about it—as a personal favor to me, don't you know."

"Hm," I'd have said, "about my will in all of what, exactly?"

Dracula: In all that's about to happen (*brushing imaginary lint from his sleeve and clearing his throat*) ... between us, that is.

Me: Ahh, I see. But what about you? How does *your* "will" fit into all this?

Dracula: (*shrugging his shoulders*) My will is not exactly what you'd call an issue for me these days.

Me: Oh, right. But I still don't get why you want this whole thing to look like it's my idea ...

D: Well if you're going to make a big thing of it ...

Me: Hey, I'm only asking.

D: (*leaning over, whispering confidentially*): Listen, dear, just try and lighten up for once, why don't you? This isn't Milwaukee—this is Transylvania. We do things differently here.

Me: Yeah, I know, but…

D: Oh, for heaven's sake! Can't you just for once in your life try and fit in? This isn't very attractive, you know, this paranoia of yours. But I guess I should have known you'd be just like the rest of your family, all screwed up and nervous about every little thing.

Me: Hey, wait a second—how'd we get from "your custom" to "my family?"

D: *(turns back, crosses arms)* Forget it. Just forget I asked.

Me: Yeah, well… I think I'll be going now.

D: *(snapping angrily)* Of course you will! You always run away from anything you can't handle.

Me: (*signaling the coachman as I start down the steps*) Yeah, okay, whatever you say…

D: You always have to have everything your own way. Selfish—that's you!

Me: (*fluttering fingers over my shoulder*) Uh-huh, well then. *Bye!*

D: *(suddenly calm, nods head knowingly)* You'll be back. You need me! (*Then inside, slamming door behind himself and stomping his foot*) *Shit!*

If by some chance we're not taken in by our vampires' initial efforts to shift responsibility to us by their usual means of deception and fast-talking, they're apt to resort to a crueler means of persuasion.

Like Dracula, our practical vampires will try to weaken and get us off balance. And just like the rest of us in the heat of an argument, our vampires will let fly just about anything they can lay their hands to, including personal insults about:

Our competence: lack of education/ability/intelligence

Our morality: sins of omission/commission/selfishness

Our appearance: faults in features, weight, fitness

Our stamina: lack of strength, speed, vigor

Our humanity: unworthiness of being treated with respect and common dignity

In particular, they can use *any of these things we've confided to them that we're insecure about as weapons:* our families, friends, jobs, and affiliations are popular targets, too.

Anything that provides us with a personal source of strength, love, or growth will always be a favorite point of attack for our vampires. If we have a supportive best friend, she'll be labeled stupid, crazy, or immoral. If we have a favorite hobby, association, or outside interest of *any* kind it will be judged (a) a ridiculous waste of time, (b) totally selfish, or, most likely, (c) both.

If there is anything in our lives supportive or enriching, our vampires will immediately perceive it as a threat and rush to advise us of its flaws. If it looks like those supportive or enriching things might increase the breathing space between our vampires and us, we can bet our vampires will rush to bleed them. You see, those positive things turn our attention and energy away from our vampires' needs, and they definitely don't want us pursuing things that make us better and stronger.

Our family of origin is surely a favorite vein for our vampires to penetrate. The tiniest sip or subtlest prick to this particular vein initiates the flow of heart's blood: blood from our most central and intimate source.

You saw the way Dracula tried to dig into my family back there, accusing them of being *"All screwed up and nervous about every little thing."* By attacking my family, he attempted to suck from the very source of my life, to drain me of confidence in my origin, my birthright, and—as vernacular coincidence would have it—my *blood*.

We want to be especially alert to vampires who show contempt for our pedigree or disapproval of the people and experiences that made us who we are today. Vampires who attack our essence that way are serious about their feeding, and often seem able to take "the heart" right out of us.

But that's vampire technique for you: a little nip here, a tiny bite there—it keeps the blood draining and our constitutions weak. These little wounds can make a big difference to a hungry and controlling vampire, and keeping us in a slightly injured and weakened state is just good dining insurance for them. We're far less likely than "fresher" hosts are to fight back and besides, when we're feeling fragile and scared, we're almost never thinking about our invitations, much less our power to revoke them. All we're thinking about is our vampire's next meal, and what an unpleasant experience it's going to be for us.

Internalized Solicitations

A friend was telling me about how she'd been nearly crippled recently with anxiety about a social gathering that she and her husband were planning to attend. The party consisted of a group of friends they've known and loved for years, but there was a tendency among some members to gossip. She explained to me how certain members of the group often "constructively criticized" any member not in attendance when they gather, and how she was so worried she'd been the most recent subject of their "analysis" she was losing sleep over it.

I didn't like it. These sounded to me like vampires that might once have lived "outside" of her—by which I mean that her anxiety about them was at one time triggered only by being in their physical company—but had moved "inside," and she was now carrying her anxiety about them around with her. Her worry was starting to feed on her even when they weren't around—proof that they were living on the inside, which is just about the worst place possible for them to be hanging out.

When a friend tells me she's been waking up repeatedly in the middle of the night worrying about her friends criticizing her behind her back, it tells me that her vampires have moved from outside to inside; that they've taken up residence inside her in a way that no bum on the street or telemarketer over the phone could ever do. It speaks to the seriousness of the threat we live under as hosts as we surrender our sleep, our thoughts, our time, and ultimately our lives over to our vampires' control. It's just like in those vampire movies, where the host is walking around in a daze, bewitched by a force the rest of us can't see or hear. It demonstrates that the thrall they're under has reached beyond the outside and physical presence of their vampires, and now lives within.

When our vampires and their solicitations begin living inside of us, it's fear that brings them over our inner thresholds. Maybe it's the habitual pain we suffer at the hands of our vampires that produces that fear and internalizes it in an effort to defend us—keeping us vigilant and prepared for their next attack so we can avoid being as hurt as we were the last time they fed. Or maybe the seeds of our fear were planted long before our vampires ever came into our lives, and now their repeated abuses have worked like Miracle-Gro on those fears, bringing them to full bloom inside us at the mere thought of our vampires. However it happens, it means their power over us has moved inside and they now have the ability to control us no matter what their physical distance from us might be.

There comes a point with certain vampires where we can see that they and their solicitations are beginning to dictate, more and more each day, the way we spend our time and live our lives. Lots of us are hosting the same inner vampire my friend was: a fear of being judged by others—by our friends, employers, relatives, and even by strangers sometimes, when we imagine that people we don't even know are evaluating or criticizing us as we walk through a store or down a busy street. Or maybe it's a private terror we have of losing our jobs or the ability to care for our families, concerns which, when proportionate, are healthy—but when overblown can interfere with our ability to sleep or to enjoy our lives. Such fears become vampires that dine from within, threatening to consume us entirely. Sometimes they can be in the secrets we keep or parts of our lives we're desperately trying to hide from others. They might be the lies we tell, the things we do that we're ashamed of, or the addictions we have and feel the need to keep secret until finally (because it is natural that our secrets should separate us from others) we are left feeling lonely, disconnected, and wondering in our isolation whether life has any meaning for us at all anymore.

We're wise to take these inner vampires seriously; armed with real cunning and a natural ability to work in the dark, they can easily end up determining who we are and what we do and value. If we don't snap out of their thrall and start making conscious choices about them pretty soon, we may find ourselves looking back on our lives one day, sadly realizing how much we lived for our vampires instead of ourselves, and worse, how we could have taken our lives back from them but never did.

Whether our vampires live outside us or inside us, however, we need to be sure of our diagnoses. While being able to spot their solicitations is a good start, there's more to diagnosing the presence and seriousness of our vampires than how they get in. We need to consider how they look to us and how we feel when they're feeding, too.

3

When They Bite

Examining Our Wounds—Inside and Out

I WAS CHECKING OUT AT A GROCERY store offering one of those club membership things recently, and the clerk—who has gotten to know me and knows that I am not a club member, will never become a club member, will continue to pay outrageous prices just for the pure pleasure of remaining a club non-member—said to me, "So you haven't decided to give us a made-up name or fake phone number for your account yet?"

She was referring to a scheme employed by a number of customers not wishing to have their comings, goings, and purchases recorded, who can't stand the thought of selling their privacy for the supposed savings of a few bucks: they give a false name and phone number for purposes of their own club membership.

"Nope," I told her, "that would look like compliance, and I'm not complying. It would be like a rose by any other name, you know? It would still be me."

She nodded. "You know," she said, "I'm really surprised more people don't refuse to sign up. It's really kind of weird how few people even question it."

"Well," I said, "I guess if people actually stopped to think about how much they might be inviting in when they sign up for these 'clubs,' they *would* question it. But since honest people are pretty trusting most of the time, they assume everyone else—even corporations—is being honest with them too."

"Yeah," she said, and we laughed. An identification card to buy groceries indeed! What do these vampires take us for, anyway—their next meal?

Well, they can forget it. I may not understand the full extent of what's asking to come in when I refuse solicitations like these, but I do have a pretty good idea of what a vampire looks like and how one sounds when it's trying to seduce me.

The Way a Vampire Looks and Sounds

How do we know a vampire when we see and hear it? There are of course the obvious ones for most of us: telemarketers, credit card companies, the IRS, and practically anyone we actively dislike, to name a few; these bloodsuckers aren't hard to spot. They drain our patience, time, money, energy, and good will every day. But what about some of the more subtle vampires—the ones whose fangs aren't so clearly visible, whose drinking isn't so plainly audible?

What is it, for instance, about our favorite supermarkets, drug companies, gas stations, or airlines that I'm suggesting should cause us to start nervously patting our pockets for garlic? There are no membership fees, and all we get are the benefits of savings with them and other companies they're associated with.

They promise they're not selling our names or any personal information they collect, so what's all the fuss about?

Well, keeping in mind the vampire's propensity for deception *and* the bottomless pit that is its appetite, we might begin to answer that question by examining the way one vampire-disguised-as-grocery-store looked when it made its initial approach—or rather, *solicited its invitation*—to me.

Were there colorful streamers hanging everywhere, and big bright signs pasted all over the store that first week they were introducing their offer? Was there a decorated sign-up table with lots of friendly folks there, pushing applications and fliers on customers as they walked through the doors? Were there cars clogging the parking lot and hundreds of cheerful balloons bouncing in the wind? Was practically everyone in town eagerly telling me how they'd just purchased orange juice for fifty cents a can there, and asking if I'd signed up to be a member of *the Club* too?

You bet there were, you bet there was, and you bet they did.

And while I like a party as well as anyone, I have to say that there's something about all that hoopla that just doesn't add up for me—there's something there that gives me a sneaking suspicion that they might be trying to seduce me.

I have to ask myself, when someone who's in business to make money works that hard to get my attention (and signature) right that minute, what it is they might not want me to look at or have the time to think about.

All their big bright signs and fun bouncy balloons remind me of those credit card guys with their shiny stickers and daring challenges to move their stickers from one location to another. Their rush to sign me up and the excessively innocent expressions on their faces when I ask if my personal information will be sold to or otherwise shared with allied companies reminds me of telemarketers who call me with an offer that's "free," but about to expire in the next five minutes. Their colorful signs warmly inviting me to *"Join the Club!"* that provide friendly admonitions like, *"Don't miss out!"* remind me of Dracula confidentially advising me to get with it and be like everyone else in Transylvania, or else.

At my first refusal to "join the club," the clerk, observing that I was perhaps too dumb to understand it and in need of a calmer, more personalized explanation, attempted—gently—to educate me, "You really *should* get a card, Mrs. Cunningham. I can't issue your savings without it," she said, and then waited to see if she'd finally managed to penetrate my thick skull.

Within about five seconds, though, she decided it was time to quit messing around: "It's company policy," she flatly advised me—maybe she thought a little intimidation might help move things along.

"Yeah, yeah, yeah," I thought, "I've heard this vampire rap a million times." It's always:

We just require this information to update the system.

Or: *We only utilize this data to verify our records.*

Or: *This is just for the computer.*

Oh, well, why didn't you say so? If it's just for the computer, then I'm sure it's probably too technical and important for me to understand.

But that's one of the nice things about corporate vampires: they're usually pretty easy to spot, since the way they're soliciting so often goes from charming (balloons, smiles, and stickers) to subtly threatening or enthralling (bureaucratic or intimidating language); none of it ever looks quite right.

That and the fact that the rules never change: we can always be on the lookout for their solicitation (*sign here—right now!*)

and watch for the deception (*you'll save money!*), the seduction (*be one of us!*), and the emergency (*limited time only!*) they'll be using to try and get in every time. When those strategies fail, however, and they see that they *still* can't suck an invitation out of us, their true desperation and hunger really start to show.

Whether mythological or personal, all vampires must answer to an authority greater than their own. In the movies, it's always some vampire explaining in blank, undead tones to the victim how an invitation is required because "the Master commands it." In the corporate world, "company policy" is always the Big Boss. Either way, when our vampires' sweeter and less intimidating solicitations fail, they'll drag these superiors out every time. Some of us can be pretty vulnerable to authority figures, after all.

Who, *us*? Question authority? Cause a scene? Never. Where do we sign? Would they like our checking account number, too, and our mother's maiden name? To know whether we own or rent our homes? We'll tell them anything they want to know. We're no troublemakers. We're *good*.

Only there we are a few months later, paying for that obedience and marveling over all the unwanted phone calls, junk mail, spam, and new club invitations we're suddenly receiving—to say nothing of how our grocery bills are still what they were before we joined their "savings" club.

And the moral, of course, is that if what they're offering looks a little off to us, if we feel rushed or intimidated, or if we feel we're being asked for "just one more thing" with a regularity that calls to mind that vampire-defining insatiability, we might want to pause next time any corporation or institution approaches us, and think twice about what we might be inviting in.

Lair Sweet Lair

Most of us don't even have to leave home to be solicited by a vampire; some of the hungriest we feed come to us from down the block, around the corner, and even worse, from right inside our own homes. Brr ... it's just like that old movie about the babysitter and the psycho killer who keeps calling her on the phone and asking if she's checked the children: the last time she picks up the phone it's the cops, and they're screaming, "Get out of there! We've traced the line and *he's calling from inside the house*!"

They can be pretty hair-raising, these vampires with their invitations to come and go and phone anytime they please. We live in a low-grade fever of anticipation, tensing just slightly every time the phone rings or there's a knock on the door. We experience feeling pulled against our will to answer them too—as if our feet had no choice but to walk to the door, our hand no alternative but to reach for the phone—and if that's not enthrallment, I don't know what is.

Case in Point: Ted the Joshing Vampire

Ted was a guy I used to know who came over almost every night, just as I was getting ready for supper. I was so innocent back then, I didn't even catch that he was timing it so my husband Robert wouldn't be home from work when he came. I thought the three of us were pals and it was by accident Robert wasn't home when he showed up. So, I thought it was by accident I was the one who had to visit with him too—listening to him tell the same stories and jokes over and over again, and trying to laugh or smile as I did.

Back then, I believed that because he meant no harm, I couldn't revoke my invitation to him. I thought that because he didn't know how he was hurting me, it meant I couldn't defend myself. Can you imagine? That's how naïve I was—how little I understood about the vampire rules in those days!

His pattern was to drop in late afternoons and while talking, hint and hint (and hint) about how he wanted to stay for dinner. He would act as if it was "joking," but he never let up so I would finally have to ask, "Ted, would you really like to stay for dinner?" Sometimes he would, but more often he'd just make another confusing joke that didn't answer the question and after a few months of this game, it really wore me down.

There I was, a new wife and mother trying to get everything right, trying to be kind and the best person I could be, and he was making me sick—literally—because any spare moment I might've had before I cooked dinner was sacrificed to *his* needs. He didn't really interest me or even act much like a real friend does—like someone who listens, sees your needs, and cares about them.

Sometimes he'd bring nice little things for my daughter Maddie to play with, but it wasn't long before I started thinking he was using those presents as admission (excuses) to come in, a clear sign something was wrong with the relationship.

I was in denial about him, afraid to think he might have been a vampire and even more afraid to know he was for sure. But today I'm not afraid and do know for sure. I know because of the way he indulged his own selfish need to impose on me and my time, never seeing—the way friends do—that I was busy, had a new husband and baby, and might have wanted to rest a bit before dinnertime. All he ever saw was what Ted needed and eventually I didn't want to be the person who gave up her own life to meet those needs anymore.

Guys like Ted aren't the only ones who can make us sick, though. Any person, institution, or thought we haven't identified as draining and clearly defined our limits to has the potential to become a vampire to us, but we can easily diagnose ourselves.

If you feel yourself cringe when the phone rings or there's a knock on the door, but you don't know why, then try this: Sit down, close your eyes, take a couple of calming breaths, and then quietly remember the last time you felt that way. What were you thinking when that shot of fear ran through you?

- Was there someone in particular you thought might be on the other side of that door or the other end of that phone that made you jump? Who is that person who makes you so uneasy? What's their name?
- Ask yourself what it is about that person that makes you so uncomfortable. Do you owe them money? An apology? Is there something that happened between the two of you that has never been spoken of but needs to be? Are they repeatedly disrespectful or suggestive in a way that makes you ill at ease? Do you feel your relationship with them is undefined or that the other person has different feelings for you than you do for him/her? Or have you simply never made it clear where your threshold is and that you don't want this particular person dropping in or calling any old time he or she wants?

That anxiety is there to serve us and has so much it wants to tell us about our relationships and ourselves. Besides, sooner or later our anxiety will become another bloodsucker in itself and we'll find ourselves "catching two vampires with one invitation."

More Diagnostics: The Way They Do the Things They Do

Some family members, neighbors, and friends may not necessarily *be* vampires in themselves, but the things they say and do can certainly drain us. Sadly and naturally enough, it's the people closest to us who make the greatest contributions of "constructive criticism" to the collection baskets of self-doubt most of us carry around. Although some of these people don't intend to hurt us, they are obviously blind to the futility and even cruelty of their suggestions. Their "helpful" words can leave us frustrated, hurt, and—after a while—guarded about spending any time with them at all.

Girlfriends we think we know so well can shock us practically into the next dimension when they share remarks like these with us in public:

There's a new book out by Dr. Phil I think would be just perfect for you.

You are so lucky to have a husband as handsome as yours.

There's a sale going on over at Macy's and I saw some beautiful padded bras there. You should check it out.

Husbands and partners have been known to surprise us with a few insensitive observations of their own:

My last girlfriend was really beautiful on the outside, but you're so beautiful on the inside.

You look great ... except for your face.

And my personal all-time favorite:

If you ever want a nose job, I'll be happy to pay for it.

Now *that* was confusing—I mean, it was like the person saying it was trying to be helpful but in a totally psychotic and insulting way.

There are neighbors who like to camouflage their criticism with this same kind of benevolence:

I have some extra tulip bulbs that would look just beautiful growing outside your front door.

Just say the word and I'll help you paint that garage.

Did you know the community center is now offering dog obedience classes? I think they would be perfect for you and Bowser.

It's weird—getting set up to have to say thank you for being criticized like that. However, most of us have experience with people who like to counterfeit thoughtfulness in that way: they buy us tickets to someplace we have no interest in going (their bowling tournaments in a far away state, for instance) or give us gifts we have no interest in owning (a sweater in exactly the style and color we never wear). And we all know how much they like to be thanked for doing things we don't want done: for making our dinner but leaving the mess for us to clean up, or for "remodeling" a room we haven't been able to use because they're "still working on it." We all know how it is to get stuff we never asked for and still be expected to gush with gratitude for it.

It isn't the worst sin in the world, I'll grant you, but when you add that to the fact that when we really *do* need their help or assistance—for money or compensation, for time off or help with the kids, for a particular food/item of clothing, or even medicine we need—they'll tell us what we're asking for is unreasonable and we're just plain wrong for thinking we needed it in the first place.

"Being made wrong" for every single thing we do, need, and think can make us sick, but there's something else that can make us sicker—and that's defending the vampire who's trying to make us wrong in the first place.

- Do you tell yourself that the way your vampire treats you "isn't that bad," "could be a lot worse," or is "at least better than it was before?"
- Do you make allowances for their abusive behavior because you "understand things about them that other people don't"—like maybe how much pressure they're under or how bad they had it when they were kids?
- Do you hear whispers from within, telling you that your vampires, "are probably right" in their criticism—or worse, do you hear voices speaking at full volume from within, telling you that your vampires "are *surely* right" in their criticism?

Only people who have relationships with the undead feel the need to make excuses for them that way, and only people who host vampires feel a greater need to let their vampires off the hook for all the pain they're causing them than they do to defend themselves against the infliction of that pain.

One way to diagnose the presence of a vampire in your life is by checking to see if you're putting their needs above your own—and I *don't* mean "because you love and respect them," either. I mean because you're enthralled and have forgotten how *not* to put their needs above your own. Perhaps you've forgotten you're just as worthy of love and respect as they are.

There's a difference between the love we give that brings us joy and fulfillment, and the love we give that brings us misery and self-doubt. We see the difference, we hear the difference, but still don't trust our senses. And trusting ourselves is essential to positively identifying our vampires.

A spouse or partner can take over the administration of your life, inside and out: both as manager of how you spend your days and arbiter of how much or little you value yourself. We all know how they can move in—first by getting over our thresholds, then by slowly assuming control over our activities, and eventually our thoughts and beliefs, too.

An addiction to drugs or alcohol can enter and take control in much the same way a person can. Gambling, credit card abuse, and compulsive issues around food and eating can move in and take over in a similar way. Almost anything can become a vampire to us if we extend an invitation to it. And once they're vampires, you'll probably notice that all *their* needs and entitlements usually come before your own.

But our vampire might be of a smaller and less dominating class. It might be that crazy-making next-door neighbor or coworker we have, the one who doesn't consume *vats* of our blood in the way an abusive partner or an addiction does, but just a small vial or two of it each day instead.

No matter how we might mistrust what our eyes and ears tell us, and no matter how we try to hide from our suspicions— that our partner doesn't really mean to be cruel, that we still have control over our alcohol or drug use, or that the coworker who's driving us nuts isn't a big deal—there is one diagnostic measure we cannot change or hide from. There is one way to the truth about our vampires we cannot push away intellectually, because our *intellect* is not where it lives.

Looking Within

Many of us, when attempting to determine the presence of a vampire in our lives, resolve to study them more carefully. We survey, measure, and evaluate *them*, searching for any clues we can find as to what they really are: friend or foe. We take note of their deceptions, their inconsistencies, their exploitations, and their appetites, doing our best to objectively record what we suspect might be vampirish characteristics. We calmly ask ourselves whether they're showing that they truly love or value us, or if they are in fact, only feeding on us. The more we look and listen, the closer we come to concluding that they must be vampires. We tell ourselves, with dismal satisfaction, that we're seeing the truth about them for the first time.

When we gather this data and try to analyze it, however, we feel ourselves beginning to falter. Our results seem inconclusive and our old doubts and reservations resurface, even in the face of the overwhelming evidence we just collected. We wonder if we could have been mistaken. We tell ourselves we're being unfair. Our fear of making an irreversible mistake prevents us from embracing a final conclusion and it seems there's no way for us to be absolutely sure if we've got a real vampire feeding or not.

Here's the thing that kills me, though: When a dog bites us, we don't *look at the dog* to see how badly we've been hurt, we *look at the bite*. When I was seven years old and a basenji named Sheba removed an ounce of flesh from the palm of my hand, you'd better believe I didn't screw around trying to get a closer look at her to see whether she was really a dog or not—I pulled my hand away as quick as I could to get a closer look at where she bit me!

It's ironic that when most of us start suspecting a vampire has bitten us, the first thing *we* try to do is to get a closer look at the *vampire*. It's as if by confirming that it's really a vampire, we're allowed to believe our wounds are genuine and therefore really painful! Or as if, by confirming it's really not a vampire, we can believe our wounds are superficial and therefore less painful!

A thorough diagnosis of our personal vampires requires that we search not only outside ourselves where we can study the vampire, but also inside ourselves where we can measure the injury it's done. Determining the authenticity of a vampire requires much more than simply evaluating the way it looks and sounds; it also requires analyzing how our wounds feel.

Analyzing the Bite

Fear: This is one of our most definitive wounds, usually showing up as general feelings of anxiety and foreboding almost always compounded by something much more specific: the sickening dread we feel about our vampire's next feeding or possible ambush. There are times we can predict their appetites and mealtimes, but there are other times we can't—when their feedings are calculated to ambush and thus keep us off balance, and that secret schedule magnifies our fear by ... oh, maybe about a thousand times.

Despair: Occurs when we start believing there's no point in trying to escape our vampire and that we're powerless to change our circumstances. This is probably the most tender of our wounds, as you may already know, and one that's easily identified by the depth and breadth of plain old sadness we feel.

Doubt/Guilt/Envy: These are also pretty common wounds to be found on any host; the crippling doubt we have about who we are, who we're beginning to suspect our vampires are, and then (as an added bonus) the guilt we feel about having those doubts and about the secrets we're keeping from our truly loving friends and family with regard to those doubts. On top of these, there is the envy or jealousy we sometimes feel as a result of our low self-esteem and self-doubt.

Loneliness: Keeping those secret doubts and the truth about our suspicions isolates us, and the more of ourselves we think we have to hide, the deeper into the dark we'll go and more alone we'll feel.

Starvation: That's what it feels like: the deprivation we feel every time we're faced with our vampires' ingratitude and infuriating need to absolve themselves of any responsibility they have for their appetites and behaviors. We starve for want of love, respect, recognition, the tiniest bit of old-fashioned fair play, or even just a simple "thank you." And the longer we live without those things, the more we really do begin to feel as if we're starving.

Resentment: Good old everyday resentment—and I do mean every day. I'm referring to the anger we feel toward a certain person, institution, situation, or belief in our lives that occurs over and over again. It's an anger that returns with such regularity, in fact, that it starts to feel like a normal part of our lives, a vampire we interact with and feed daily without even thinking twice. I can remember, for instance, driving to a job I used to have. Every morning and right on schedule, about fifteen minutes into the trip it would come: my resentment about a certain coworker and my obsessive thinking about what she was going to say and do that day and the script I had for how

> I was really going to tell her off this time. Honestly, it was the same performance in my mind every morning: she'll say this, I'll say that; she'll do this, I'll do that—all the way to work.
>
> Our resentments might be as small but redundant as the fact that we're the only person in the house who seems to know how to empty the dishwasher or hang up our coat when we come home. Or they might be as sneaky and mean as our inner critics, telling us how awful we look every morning when we get dressed: pedestrian but deadly.

When we're searching for our resentments, this is the kind of thing we're looking for: the angry feelings we have that are so repetitive, they start to seem about as normal to us as brushing our teeth. And just like brushing our teeth, they generally come on schedule: the same resentment triggered by the same stimulus, every time.

Time to Write

When you're ready to consider yours, you'll want to make a list so you can see, in black and white, outside of you, what's going inside of you. Grab a notebook and good pen, go someplace you can be alone for a while, and then sit back and think about your day. It can be today or yesterday—either one will work. Close your eyes and pretend you're watching a movie of that day and yourself as you went through it. As you're watching, write these things down: the people, situations, and thoughts you have that make you feel frightened, despairing, lonely, doubtful, starving, invisible, or resentful. Here is a three-step process:

1. Write down the name of the person or thing that is bothering you.

2. Write down the thing they do or what happens that causes your wound.
3. Write down, *specifically,* the way your wound makes you feel.

To keep your thoughts organized, try scratching out a few simple columns, making a list that looks something like this:

PERSON OR SITUATION (THE VAMPIRE)	WHAT THEY DO/ WHAT HAPPENS (THE BITE)	HOW I FEEL (THE WOUND)
My Neighbor	Drops in without warning, talks about the same problems she's had forever over and over again, takes up much of my time and energy, borrows my belongings and money.	*Invisible/Resentful*—she doesn't respect my time or needs and she takes my loans of belongings and money for granted and doesn't show appreciation. *Guilty/Doubtful*—she's so needy I feel I'm never doing enough for her. *Fearful/Anxious*—I never know when she'll pounce/come over/ask for something.
My Spouse/ Partner	Refuses to acknowledge the money I make or the work I do, leaves his/ her stuff all over the house, never says thank you, and never tells me that he/she thinks I'm attractive, makes me feel bad about my drinking and tries to control it—accuses me of being alcoholic.	*Invisible/Resentful*—he/she thinks they contribute more to our marriage/ partnership than I do. *Starving*—he/she never acknowledges the work I do or says thank you. *Despairing/Lonely*—he/she doesn't care about my feelings and no longer loves me. *Afraid*—fear he/she will leave me and that I won't be attractive to anyone else. *Resentful/Afraid/Doubtful*—angry he/ she never looks at their own faults and makes me feel ashamed; afraid they may leave me, interferes with my drinking, and I may have a problem and have to stop; doubtful because I don't want to believe drinking is a problem and sometimes it seems manageable.

(Continued on next page)

(continued)

Person or Situation (The Vampire)	What They Do/ What Happens (The Bite)	How I Feel (The Wound)
My Coworker	Talks about me behind my back to other employees and boss, takes credit for work I've done and ideas I've had, makes more money than I do, is younger and better-looking than me.	*Resentful/Doubtful*—I don't want to sink to his/her level and gossip about them, and I'm not sure how much of what I'm afraid of is true. *Afraid*—I might lose my job/financial security. *Invisible/Starving*—my manager can't see how hard I'm working. *Envious/Resentful*—I'm not as good-looking as the coworker is and not as well liked because of it.

Bring these things into the light where you can see them; that's as far as you go for now. There will be more to do later, of course, but as *practical* slayers, we take this one step at a time, in the order prescribed, with thoroughness, and without skipping any steps.

There's a fabulous scene in *'Salem's Lot* where the slayers are driving all over town, finding all the vampires' hiding places and marking them with a big black grease pencil. Their plan is to *find* all the vampires first, then slay them later on—for efficiency's sake, as I recall—because they don't have a lot of time.

When they find a vampire hiding under a porch (the soles of its work boots give it away), one of them gets the idea of trying to pull it out into the daylight to see if that might be enough to kill it. The others agree it's worth a try, and so they start heaving this vampire out from under the porch where it's hiding.

But is this the big and dramatic solution we hope it will be, where the vampire bursts into flames or crumbles into ash when it hits the light?

It's not. First the vampire starts to steam—more like wet laundry than anything else—and then it starts to twitch and kick.

The skin pulls away from its teeth, revealing their new shape, and then it starts to hunch and squirm its way blindly back under the porch. It's a scene not so much exciting or spectacular as it is plain old revolting.

The slayers stand there and watch until it's finally wormed its way back into the dark and lies still again, then, slightly sickened, they mark the spot with their grease pencil and prepare to go on. This, of course, is the moment they understand it's going to take a lot more to slay their vampires than just dragging them into the light: it's going to take real work and dedication.

When we make this list, we're doing exactly the same thing: we're dragging our vampires into the light and marking down where they hide. Creating this list is not "slaying," but we also know now that if they wiggle back under the porch, we'll be able to find them again. Now that we've seen them clearly, we know exactly what they look like and where they live.

Diagnostics and Three I's to Remember: Invisibility, Insatiability, and Ingratitude

There is another diagnostic tool we have, and it relates to the feeling of invisibility we sometimes get around our vampires and how that ties into our vampires' failure to acknowledge the things we do for them. Do you remember when Dracula said to Mr. Harker:

"Enter freely, and of your own will."

Predators like Dracula don't say things like that *only* because they don't want to take responsibility for their invitations, although that's a very big part of it. Underneath, there is a reason they wait for us to make all the decisions, sit quietly until we suggest solutions to their problems, and a reason they won't simply ask for what they want. There's a reason they wait for offers of food, shelter, and assistance, and it's the same reason they don't want to be held accountable for any pain or inconvenience they cause us, as well.

It's because they're proud.

Vampires don't *like* having to clean up after themselves or having to say they're sorry. They don't like to admit they make mistakes and that's why they won't make decisions, either; they might have to take responsibility for making the wrong one. They don't like to humble themselves by having to ask for things directly and they certainly don't want to appear to need anyone. They don't want to cooperate, to be an equal partner in any relationship, or to be a peer in any community, either. But more than anything else, vampires do not like having to say thank you.

There's a magical thing that happens when we express gratitude for things we've been offered in this life: *we receive them*. When we fail to acknowledge something we've been given by withholding gratitude, we cannot accept or retain it: it's as if our ingratitude dismisses that thing, and as a result we never receive it.

This dismissal is what makes for insatiable appetites and everlasting hunger: no matter how much they're offered or how much they take, vampires can never receive any of it because they refuse to acknowledge or say thank you. And if they never receive a meal—no matter how many servings they demand—they'll never be anything but hungry and dissatisfied, and will always do their best to trick us into giving them more.

But the sad truth is that many vampires don't have to trick us into providing what they want or even hint at it, because so many of us take pride in being able to read their minds and anticipate their appetites. For some of us it's actually part of the contract: we begin our relationships, right at the starting gate, with the understanding that we will always provide whatever the other person needs without their having to ask, acknowledge it, or thank us for it. Sometimes we began with people who *tried* to thank us for the things we did, but we—priding ourselves on being the perfect hosts—immediately established a "no gratitude" clause in our contracts by saying, "Oh, no need to thank me," or "it was nothing"—which actually encouraged these people to hurt and ignore us.

The trouble with never receiving acknowledgment or gratitude is that we can start to feel as if we're disappearing and eventually feel like we're not even here at all. Remember when we discussed how we become invisible to our vampires and how their blindness makes it impossible for them to see our needs? They're not always alone in that blindness, and if we're not careful, we'll become invisible to ourselves, too.

There's a most heartbreaking and frankly amazing description of what can happen in the relationship between hosts and mirrors in *'Salem's Lot*. I've never seen this subject handled in vampire literature anywhere else, and it certainly bears reviewing. The scene concerns a young vampire boy's mother who has been hosting her son every night since his supposed death: this poor woman is weak, dazed, and completely worn out, but doesn't know why. She has no conscious memory of her son's nightly feedings on her, recalling them only as dreams.

She's talking with her husband one morning, telling him about the night before in their bathroom when she'd barely been able to make out her own reflection in the mirror. She explains how her image was so faint, she could almost see straight through it to the objects reflected in the room behind her: like she could see the bathtub and shower curtain in the mirror, but not herself.

This is what happens when we host a vampire for too long, and even when we're hosting them out of love, as this woman was with her son—when we keep telling ourselves that "we can handle" our vampire's feedings just a little longer. Not only do we become dangerously ill from all the "blood-loss" (loss of self), but there also comes a point where we almost can't see what's left of ourselves to save. Our own reflections start to disappear, and pretty soon we cease to exist—as the mirror implies, especially to ourselves.

It's the constancy of the feedings that gets us eventually: the feedings we courteously pretend aren't occurring, the "anemia" that causes our confusion, and the absence of gratitude and acknowledgment for all we do in our diligence to be perfect hosts that wears us down completely, and makes us feel like we might never see ourselves again.

No wonder we feel invisible. Vampires are a tricky, hungry bunch that know the rules and will always try to prevent us from remembering who we are and where our power really is.

Ask the Slayer

WHAT'S UP WITH MY SISTER VAMPIRES?

Dear PVS,

Why are some women vampires to other women? I know so many who are nice to your face but backbiting the second you turn around. How come?

Signed,
Baffled in S.F.

Dear San Francisco,

It's funny how many women have friends they don't trust at all. I'm shocked when they tell me about their two-faced girlfriends, and always think, "*Why would you want to be friends with someone like that anyway?*"

It sounds like you've asked yourself this question and already made the choice to find more satisfying relationships, so good for you!

But to answer your question, I think for many women it's simply politics: the social politics of feeling we need to be friendly with one woman because she's also a friend of another friend of ours. Then there are politics at work: where we have to interact with some woman for forty hours a week and try to keep the relationship as pleasant as possible, no matter how backbiting she may be.

I'm no expert on feminism, but there are plenty of books out there that might answer your question. As a practical vampire slayer I have the same solution for all difficult relationships, whether with men or women: we bring light to them so we can make clear decisions about who we are, who we want to be involved with, and to what degree. The beauty of bringing these relationships into the light is that they then no longer victimize us. We know we've made a choice and have thus restored our personal power.

PVS

....

4

A Word About Power

From Buffy Herself

I'VE NOTICED THAT MANY OF US WHO'VE been hosting vampires for a while can get all mixed up about the business of power and who's got it. It is not my wish to hurt anyone's feelings, of course, but I do feel I should point out that when a vampire has been draining us for weeks or months or even years, we are not necessarily at our "mental best" and are therefore susceptible to all sorts of silly ideas. One silly idea most of us are exposed to with sickening regularity and considerable force is this idea that our vampires have all the power, and that we don't have any. Isn't that always the way with vampires? It's like they have this mantra they have to repeat again and again about how strong and wise and superior *they* are, and how weak and dopey and second-rate *we* are.

Like any good salespeople, controlling vampires understand the value of frequent repetition. This explains why so many of them are faithful to a regular schedule of condescending and even brutal remarks to us. As hosts, we routinely get an earful of their comprehensive criticism, whether, as the saying goes, "we need it or not." Their lies and exaggerations are precisely tailored to fit our own fears and doubts about ourselves, and are, in fact, custom-made just for us.

My friend Paula once came to me about her husband, whom she described as being *publicly* mild-mannered but privately vampire-mannered. She was terrifically gorgeous—an intelligent and energetic middle-aged woman—and this was the second marriage for both her and her husband. They'd been together for about fifteen years when she confessed to me that she was starting to get pretty annoyed with what had first seemed like a merely childish habit of his.

She said that every time he could find a way to weave it into conversation, he would talk about how he had "molded her into a new woman" since they'd married. He liked to remind her of how he'd introduced her to hiking, canoeing, biking, and camping, and he seemed to want to take credit for making her a more complete person—sort of like Henry Higgins did with Eliza Doolittle. But she told me that even though this husband was privately and emotionally abusing her, her first husband had publicly and in every way abused her—which made this second one seem, by comparison, "not that bad."

How many times had I heard that story? Where a host goes from feeding one vampire who eats like a pig to one who eats a little more daintily, and the host thinks, because of this supposed improvement, that they shouldn't complain.

How many times? *Hundreds.* I'm not kidding.

What Paula wanted to know was how, in the first place, her husband *always* seemed to know exactly what words to use and where to aim them so they would hurt her most, and how, in spite of the fact that the things he said made her feel terrible, she was still afraid of losing him. It was a mystery to her that she could feel so hurt and still want to be with him at the same time; it didn't make sense.

How did he know, she asked me, that it was her age, her ability to interact socially, her creative potential, and her intelligence she was most insecure about? How could he criticize her about all those things so cruelly, and in the end, still manage to make her feel as though she needed him?

Paula is a textbook host, I must say. And her husband is a textbook vampire. I've heard this story before—every part of it. It illustrates a couple of principles about power I think we should discuss.

Isolated Repetition

Verbal battering works. If we hear a thing often enough and especially if it's the *only* thing we hear, sooner or later we're sure to start believing it ourselves. Paula's husband managed to keep her attention primarily on him by living on the outskirts of town and mingling infrequently and with only a very few "choice" people—*his* choice, of course. Then too, he was always careful to stick to the same degrading themes: how she was getting old, had always been awkward, had no imagination, wasn't very smart, and the ever-popular "I've-done-so-much-to-enrich-your-life-you'd-be-nothing-without-me" routine. The result? A carefully balanced diet of isolation and repetition.

Privacy

For all the terrible defects he found in her, though, this guy, like so many of his kind, never ever suggested she get professional or outside help of any kind to fix them. There's nothing unusual about that, by the way—this type is always very careful to remind us that what goes on between them and us is *private*, and that absolutely no one else must know about it. No sharing with others, no second opinions, no way.

"This is nobody's business but ours," they'll tell us.

"It's a family matter," they'll say.

They consider it very important to keep their hosts cut off and all to themselves by these extreme measures. We've all heard the expression "divide and conquer," and it's a strategy our vampires know well: they can divide us from the people who love us and the things that strengthen us and keep us feeling connected, thus, conquering us is that much easier.

A Few Things to Look For

If you think you might be hosting a vampire that has you believing you need [them] more than [they] need you, or if you suspect your vampire is turning the tables and trying to make you believe *you're* feeding on *them* (another popular ploy), you may want to check the following list to see if any of these are true:

- You're *physically* isolated: you live in a remote area or at least far enough from the action that you need a car to get anywhere.
- You're *emotionally* isolated: you're discouraged from having more than one or two friends—if that—and your oppressor is highly critical of your family, your teachers or employers, your neighbors, and any friends you had before you became involved with them—although publicly, of course, they are friendly and courteous to all. Above all, these guys want to look *normal*.
- You are discouraged and even prevented from working or going to school—or, if you must work or go to school,

you hear a lot of criticism about the quality of the job or school you go to and any people you're naïve enough to tell your vampire you interact with. Nothing's ever good enough for them—not even a fabulous salary or straight A's on your report card.

- You don't have decent transportation, and when your car breaks down, you're dependent on your vampire to have it fixed. When that happens, they will either stall about having it fixed (saying they can't afford it, don't have the time, will get to it later, or forgot to buy the part again) or simply tell you it cannot be fixed at all.
- You don't have any money of your own and are positioned (by obstacles involving child care, transportation, or because you've been duped by one of any thousands of other excuses your vampire has given for why you have to stay home) in such a way that you cannot work to earn your own money without having to leave your relationship entirely and start again somewhere else, new and alone—which is nearly impossible, of course, because you don't have any money and have been cut off from friends and family for so long that you're afraid to ask anyone for help.
- Your vampire has an uncanny ability to bite you exactly where it hurts. He or she has discovered your areas of "thinnest skin," knows all your worst self-doubts and fears, and precisely where to attack.
- You believe them when they suggest, either directly or indirectly, that you are not strong enough, smart enough, good-looking enough, talented enough, dedicated enough, moral enough, or *sane* enough to hold a job, finish school, or have friends. They say that you're

defective—and there's a little vampire inside of you that believes them.

- You question your sanity and/or emotional health: your vampires may trick, startle, or otherwise set you up to think you're going crazy or you're somehow more neurotic than every other person out there is.

Which, by the way, I'm going to stop here to say you're **not**. You're no crazier than anybody else and if you don't know that yet, I certainly hope you will by the time you're done with this book: you are not crazy. Or defective. And above all: you are not powerless either; you just need to get straight about your vampires and whether or not you want to continue living with them. And it's my guess is that spending your life around people who want you to feel bad about yourself is probably *not* what you came here to do.

There's the vampire's point of view to consider: as far as they're concerned, almost anything can happen out there in the real world. If they don't keep us isolated, then we could be exposed to all kinds of exciting, or worse, *liberating* influences. What if we should begin to form an ambition or purpose of our own, beyond simply trying to keep their appetites satisfied?

Vampires trying to maintain the illusion of their host's dependence on them cannot have those hosts running around all over the place, meeting all kinds of cool people and doing all kinds of interesting things that might accidentally result in some kind of personal growth or independence. Somebody out there might have a *different* opinion to share with that host and alter their self-perception—maybe in a more positive light. No vampire in the world is going to sit still for self-esteem building like that! For vampires, there must be no dissolution of the message; their evaluation of us is the one that counts, and *only* theirs.

This process of destroying our self-worth by privately and systematically taking blood from our areas of thinnest skin serves the vampire in at least two ways that I can think of:

1. It reinforces in us the necessary belief that we, as hosts, deserve nothing better than our gloomy and thankless occupations as vampire chow.
2. It serves as a reminder to us that only *our vampires* have the needed expertise to appraise our lives, and that our opinions (or anybody else's) don't actually count.

As hosts to these often-persuasive vampires, it can feel as if we've surrendered our prerogatives—as if the days of making our own decisions and evaluating our own lives are far behind us, like a dream we can barely remember. It's a thing that happens slowly, one little acquiescence at a time, until the day finally comes when we awaken and wonder whatever happened to our plans to grow up and become something—*anything*—other than servants to these selfish and ungrateful vampires.

Waking Up

While waking up to the fact that we're giving our lives away to vampires may not *feel* like such a good thing, let me assure you: it is. To those of us who have awakened to the fact but still feel some doubt about our power—thanks to a combination of blood loss and a steady flow of spiteful fiction from our vampires—I'd like to offer the following *aide memoire*, a principle Buffy the vampire slayer reveals to a group of slayer-trainees, fundamental to understanding our vampires, our situations, and especially ourselves.

Here is what she tells her students:

The bad guys always go where the power is.

Let's stop for a moment and think about that, though. Because if it's true that we're so small and stupid and dependent, and that our vampires are all so big and smart and powerful, then *why* are they spending all their way-important, much-better-than-we-are time with *us*, anyway?

If they're so sharp and sophisticated and superior, why do they keep knocking on *our* doors, especially when what we have to offer is so completely inferior and distasteful and obviously unsatisfactory to them?

Frankly, from the way they talk, you'd think they'd be ashamed to solicit our second-rate invitations, much less lower themselves to feed on such common blood as ours, right?

Maybe we should ask them:

Say, I was just wondering: since I'm such
a loser and weakling, why don't you go and
find someone more worthy to feed on?

Oh wait, don't tell me. I think I got it: Could it be because we're really *not* just a bunch of losers and weaklings? Could it be that the reason our vampires keep coming back to feed on us is because we really *are* worthwhile, and in fact have much more power than we realize? Is it possible that what Buffy says is true, that *the bad guys always go where the power is*? And could it be that if they're coming to us, then *we must be where the power is*, too?

Think about it: If *we* have the wherewithal to see what they need before they even have to ask for it *and* the ability to supply those needs without so much as an ounce of acknowledgment or gratitude in return; and if, on top of that, we also have the strength to survive in spite of being isolated and subject to their constant feedings and humiliations, then maybe it *is* true. Maybe the bad guys really *do* go where the power is, and maybe they're coming to us not because we're so pathetically weak, but because we're so fantastically strong.

It certainly makes more sense than any of that nonsense our vampires have been trying to hand us about how helpless and pitiful and dependent *we're* supposed to be on *them*. Like they'd actually be hanging around to feed where there's nothing left to eat. Please.

Let me tell you something: vampires may be weak in many ways, but they are definitely not stupid. What we need to remember is that if we've got someone feeding on us and constantly on our case about all the power we supposedly don't have, it is *not* because we have no power. That's what they want us to believe, of course, but that's not the rule. The rule is that these bad guys always go where the power is—so it naturally follows that if one of them is soliciting our invitation, then we must be where the power is.

This isn't personal; it's just the rules. And if you insist on believing, after all this, that you are still an exception to the rule and don't have any power, then excuse me if this sounds unkind, but it confirms what I've been trying to tell you all along: you're just another victim of a carefully orchestrated vampire snow job.

There's really no getting around this one. A vampire simply cannot feed where there's nothing left to eat.

So the next time our vampires try to give us another line about what zeroes we are, we can simply and sweetly say to them (and ourselves),

Now listen, honeypants, that is just a
bunch of crap, and we both know it.

Because *we* know where the power is, no matter what they say.

5

Crossing the Threshold

Extending Our Invitations and the Reluctant Host

PLEASE UNDERSTAND THAT I AM NOT ADVOCATING any sort of vampire paranoia, nor am I suggesting we start sprinkling holy water over all our friends just to play it safe. Practical vampire slaying is not about hyper-vigilance, and our invitations are certainly not bad things. On the contrary: Our invitations provide us with the extraordinary ability to usher new ideas, people, services, and agreements into our lives every day. In one form or another, our invitations give consent to the possibilities outside our lives to cross our thresholds and come in.

It might be a new magazine subscription we've invited in or a new carpool arrangement for our kids; it could be a relative needing a place to stay, or a new romance. Maybe it's a new club or religion, a fresh philosophy, or a different way of treating ourselves. Our invitations bring all these things into our lives—and usually with our very best intentions, too.

When we invited that "no-risk" subscription to *Getting the Most Perfect Body Ever* magazine in, we probably thought it would help us take better care of ourselves and improve our self-esteem. When we gave the nod to that carpool with some of the other grade school parents, we hoped it might improve community relations and save us a little time and money on gas. When we invited our brother-in-law to stay, it was out of simple love and a healthy sense of familial responsibility. As far as new romances, untried clubs or religions, and fresh ideas about how to take care of ourselves go, hey, how exciting would our lives be if we never opened the door to any of that stuff? When you think about it, extending invitations is what life is really all about.

But you know how it goes, sometimes our invitations work out pretty well for us and sometimes they don't. Sometimes the new magazine is just the thing we needed to get motivated, and other times it's a monthly reminder of our physical inadequacies, complete with glossy pictures. Sometimes the car pool invites exactly the kind of camaraderie, extra time, and financial relief we were hoping for into our lives, and other times it just opens the door to some screwy parent who's always calling us with her emergency situations and special requests. Sometimes the brother-in-law we invited to stay with us actually says thank you and leaves within a reasonable length of time, and other times we're lucky if we can just get him out of the bathroom once in a while. That's the chance we take when we want to keep our lives interesting, though, because it's often hard to evaluate just who or what we've invited in until after we've had some time to get better acquainted with it.

When the result of our invitation is something profitable or pleasing to us, it's easy to admit we opened the door ourselves.

"Yes," we humbly confess, "those were our invitations."

But when we begin to suspect these are vampires we've invited in, suddenly we've never even heard of our humble invitations!

"What a stupid magazine!" we grumble when it comes.

"Where does that woman get her nerve?" we marvel when she calls.

"When's he ever going to get a job and move out?" we regularly (but quietly) groan.

And above all: "How did we ever get ourselves mixed up in *this*?" we want to know.

It seems that many of us would rather be seen as helpless victims—as nice guys being taken advantage of by the big, bad vampires—than as conscientious guardians of our own homes, keepers of our own gates with the power to extend and revoke our invitations at will.

Why do we resist possession of this magnificent power to transform our lives? What is it with us, anyway?

Well, one reason might be that we don't like to admit having poor judgment: People might think we're stupid. It's like we're afraid they'll say, "What do you mean, you 'didn't know it was a vampire' when you invited it in? The fangs, the pale skin, that silly accent—what part of *vampire* didn't you get?"

After all, they knew that magazine offer was a just another marketing trick—they could see that coming a mile away! And as for that woman in our carpool, they could have told us that she was going to turn out to be a psycho, too—hadn't we heard about her? When it comes to out-of-work brothers-in-law needing places to stay, it had certainly been obvious to them that he would fasten himself to our toilet seats for all eternity. *They* could have predicted all of this. Just how naïve are we, anyway?

Yeah, that's just what we need when we've got vampire suctioned to our necks: a lecture from our friends on how stupid we were for letting them clamp on in the first place.

But our fear about looking foolish isn't the only good reason we have for keeping mum about our invitations, because if logic tells us anything, it tells us that if we admit we invited our vampires in, then we'll probably be expected to take responsibility for throwing them out. And we just hate it when we have to pull ourselves together and tell somebody to hit the road.

For one thing, I don't like confrontation. It makes me nervous. And for another, I'm not even sure what I'm supposed to say. Usually by the time I recognize it's a vampire I'm dealing with, I'm too angry to speak at all—and I already know what a blubbering fool I become every time I try to talk when I'm mad: first I lose control of my lips, then my mind goes blank and I completely lose track of the important point I was going to make in the first place. Let's face it: I'm just no good at telling people how I really feel. And I'm not the biggest fan of telling them anything that might make them emotional, either.

What if they get mad and say mean things to me? Or worse, what if they get mad and say mean things to other people about me, and then all those people get mad at me, too? There are times when it just seems like a better idea to let my vampire feed for a while and then work something else out later. Which I will, sooner or later when the time is right. Another day.

Besides, it's only fair: I don't care if the mess the vampire made *is* in my house—it's still the vampire's mess and I'll walk around it forever to prove I'm right if I have to. Those crooks at that magazine should never have started charging me for what was supposed to be "a no-risk offer" in the first place! That nut from the carpool should have the courtesy and common sense to stop calling and expecting me to fix it every time she has a problem! And that freeloader in my guest room should have the decency and wherewithal to find his way to the door without my having to draw him a map! I don't see why I should have to do all the work when they're the ones causing all the trouble. Can't these people behave themselves without my having to tell them explain it to them? It's not my job.

Opportunity

For all the trouble they cause, though, these predators *can* make excellent scapegoats. The right vampire can supply us with a perfect alibi for being late, being tired, being broke, disengaged, nervous or upset, or just all-around unmanageable. If we're doing something in a less than perfect manner, you can just about bet it's our vampires' fault. And more than that, our vampires have got us so stressed out that we just have to:

(Check applicable boxes)

- ❑ Smoke
- ❑ Drink/drug
- ❑ Overeat
- ❑ Overspend
- ❑ Skip work
- ❑ Lose our temper
- ❑ Gossip/criticize
- ❑ Other

"Please," we tell our friends, "Get off my back about my *(temper, overeating, smoking)* vice of the week! Isn't it plain to see that this *(unwanted houseguest, annoying acquaintance, unfair debt)* vampire of the week has got me stressed out and I can't possibly be expected to behave responsibly right now? Give me a break!" we tell them.

You have to admit: these bloodsuckers can come in pretty handy when we feel the need to misbehave *and* put the blame on someone else. And as we discussed earlier, if we admit to inviting our vampire in—this person who's supposedly at the root of all our stress and unmanageability—then we'll probably be expected to show them the door, won't we? And the thing is, well, maybe some of us aren't quite ready to do that yet.

Which is okay. No matter what the reason, it's absolutely fine. We don't have to be ready to take responsibility for our invitations right this minute. Nobody says we have to anything today.

However.

There's the old saying that if you're not part of the solution, you're part of the problem. I'd like to offer a slightly different version I think fits really well here:

If I'm not a part of the problem, then there is no solution.

Get it? Like, if this mess you're in isn't at least partly the result of something you've done, then there is nothing you can *undo* to fix things. Either you're in the game or you're not. But if you're not, if you really *are* a victim and truly not a part of the problem, then heaven help you, because that means you can't be a part of the solution, either.

If you have the power to bring a magazine subscription into my life, then you also have the power to cancel it. If you have the power to invite some other parent to push past reasonable boundaries, then you have the power to push her back. And if you have the power to invite a too-needy relative into my home, then you have the power to tell them to leave, too.

Guardianship

I have a very important Watcher in my life, and her name is Jennifer. She watches over all kinds of things in my life, but more than anything else, she watches over my writing. She asked me not long ago just what was supposed to be so great about taking responsibility for our invitations. "You keep saying how important it is," she pressed, "but I'm still not sure why. What's in it for me?" she wanted to know.

My answer to her had to do with the connection between responsibility and power and about how, if we do not take responsibility for our invitations, we have no power. I told her all the good reasons we might have for not wanting to accept our responsibility and power, and then I told her about the one thing that can never come to us without them, which is *guardianship of our own lives.*

This brings us to:

Rule # 11: As guardians of our own lives, both our invitation-extending and invitation-revoking powers are exclusive. Nobody but us gets to say who or what comes in or is required to leave.

It reminds me of a phrase that many of our parents used to employ as a sort of tiebreaker when we were teenagers and our power struggles with them threatened to go on forever, to wit:

"This is my house and we go by my rules."

Remember that one? Well, that's the way it is for slayers, too—except when speaking of ourselves in a more literal sense we would actually say:

"This is my life, and my choice about how to live it."

I know it can be hard to remember at times, especially when our vampires have been feeding on us for a long time. It's almost as if our life energy is being drained into a belief that,

"My life belongs to the vampire. I only work here."

And that's a lie.

The Reluctant Host

I have been granted the gift of life. I have also been granted the gift of free will.

So have you.

Talk about a good deal.

I think there are times when we forget that these gifts belong to us—when we take them for granted and surrender them to our vampires. When I look back on my history, that's exactly what I see them feeding on. It made no difference whether the vampire was a manipulative boyfriend or a difficult employer, a relative who was giving me a hard time or a friend who was stretching the limits of my hospitality. It didn't matter whether it was my alcoholism or just some mean-talking Claudia Critic that lived inside my mind. They all fed on the same two things: they took time from my life and they prevented me from doing whatever else it was that I wanted to be doing, which means they took my free will, too.

When you get right down to it, there are only two things on the menu as far as our vampires are concerned: our lives and our will about how we want to live them. They can dress themselves up to make it look like they're soliciting for a million other things—and "shapeshifting" is one of the things vampires do best, so they're pretty good at disguising their true appetites—but when you reach the bottom line, those are the two they're after. And they just happen to be the most precious things any of us have.

No wonder they're so sought after!

No matter how we try to tell ourselves that it's okay to be hosting our vampires or that it's no big deal, that we should make allowances for them or that feeding them is our duty, there's always going to be a part of us that's just not going to buy it. There is always going to be a part of us that's seriously upset, a part that tells us it is *not* okay to give our precious lives away, and that, no matter what we think or how intimidated we may be, turning our free will over to a bunch of starved and relentless vampires is not a good idea.

Our ability to feel when something isn't good for us is a gift from our Designer, engineered and installed to work perfectly on our behalf and to our advantage. We are not designed to turn over our sacred gifts of life and free will to vampires—that's not what they're made for. They are made to thrive in light and freedom and especially in love. The reason it doesn't feel good for us to give our will and our lives over to the service of vampires is that it's *not* good for us. When our spirit finds itself wasting away under the dark thrall and bitterness of a vampire, there's a part of us inside that's there to let us know about it. We've already talked about the way it communicates: about those feelings of fear and loneliness, of doubt, envy, and guilt, of resentment and sadness, and of invisibility and despair we get. If we've made a list of who's been feeding on us and how those wounds feel, we've demonstrated to ourselves that those warnings are real and worthy of our attention.

There is a part inside of each of us that communicates with our God—the one each of us understands personally. Just as we have many names and ways of understanding God, we also we have many names and ways of understanding the part of us that connects with our God. Some call that connection "conscience" and others call it "intuition," but for our purposes and if you don't mind, I think we can simply refer to it as "the Slayer." The slayer is the one inside each of us whose job it is to communicate to us on behalf of our personal God the difference between right and wrong, between freedom and captivity, between love and fear, and between genuine charity and simply indulging a vampire. It's the part that's always been there, even when we've tried to bury it, hide from it, or replace it with something else.

About Love

I smoked cigarettes for twenty-five years, and not just a few, either. I loved smoking and everything about it—the high it gave me, the ritual it entailed, the diversion it supplied, the fire I could play with, the smell of it in the air, and eventually even the privacy it forced me to have when I could no longer smoke indoors. When I became pregnant with my daughter Madeline, I seriously tried to quit for the very first time. And I almost succeeded, except for that one or two a day I smoked at the end of my pregnancy.

When I packed to go to the hospital for her birth, I stuck my last two cigarettes into my backpack, just in case I needed them. A day or two after she was born, I pulled a cigarette and lighter out of my bag, and then wobbled outside to smoke it with one of the nurses on duty that day. When I came back into my room, Madeline was all wrapped up in a striped blanket with one of those little hats they give newborns on her head, and I wanted to pick her up but realized I couldn't. The stench and poison of cigarettes was all over me, on my hands, in my sinuses: all over, and everything about bringing that in contact with this sweet new wonder in my life felt wrong to me.

I went into the bathroom, washed my hands and face, brushed my teeth, and never smoked again—but I'll tell you something: it was really hard. When she was nine months old I still wanted to smoke so badly that I went and bought a pack—except I never opened it. As much as I'd wanted to smoke, I just couldn't bring myself to do it, and to me, that's a pretty good demonstration of the power of love and how it works.

I know how love felt when I watched my newborn daughter sleeping, and there's nothing sappy or sentimental about it: it doesn't make me want to cry or sing or any of that Hollywood stuff. What love like that does is sock me right into the present, with both feet on the ground—where I know the truth. Love gives me the power to move the thing that is weighing me down and choking the life out of me out of my way, and makes me free of it—but I won't pretend to you that it makes it easy, because it doesn't. What it does, though, is gently transform that task from being impossible to possible—power enough for this slayer.

As slayers, we don't waste our time with imitations. The kind of power we require must be both available and personal, and we shouldn't have to look too far to find it, either. This power, as the book *Alcoholics Anonymous* so impeccably expresses it, is

"... a part of our makeup, just as much as
the feeling we have for a friend."

It took me just about forever to figure that line out after reading it. I thought for so long that the power had to be something tricky or complicated, but it's not. The feeling I have for a friend is, of course, love. And it *is* a part of my makeup.

That's the kind of power we'll have to find if we hope to slay our vampires in any real or lasting sense: the kind of power that makes freedom happen; the kind of power that admits light and truth. As a matter of fact, this power *is* light and truth.

I believe this, and the more time I spend slaying vampires and working with others to slay theirs, the surer my belief becomes. There are times I've heard people refer to their God as one that "hits them with a two-by-four" to get their attention, and I can't say that I've found that kind of picture of God to be very helpful to me. The power we're looking for is here to help us: it won't be punishing us and it sure as heck won't be hitting us with a two-by-four either ... that's not its style.

Its guidance comes from the purest love that's inside and all around us, and it won't punish us to get us moving. It simply tries to remind us by communication through our inner slayer and in feelings proportionate to the danger that surrendering our precious lives to vampires whose appetites will never be satisfied is not what we came here to do.

And we know it.

If we don't feel ready to revoke our invitations, we don't have to worry about whether we're still loved or not, because that much at least should be obvious. The warnings our God sends us should be proof enough of that love, and clearly demonstrate, that It's not about to give up and leave us just because we're slow to get the message or too scared to proceed right away. It's going to keep those warnings coming no matter what we think, because that's what it's made to do, and do perfectly, too, I might add.

I believe most of us have always known we've had a connection to this power inside us. How could any of us survive, much less exercise free will, without it? Something inside makes us move—which is power. And another something inside suggests we move this way rather than that—which is guidance.

As slayers, we want to connect the two—so our power to move will be in alignment with the part of us that actually knows which is the best way to go, and when that starts to happen, things certainly seem to have a way of making a lot more sense. We begin to feel like we belong here, and that our lives really do have meaning after all.

Which sounds just a whole lot more practical than feeding a bunch of vampires does any day.

Ask the Slayer

Denial and the Helpful Neighbor

Dear PVS,

I have a neighbor who drops over without warning at least five times a week. She pokes around and makes suggestions about the curtains she thinks I need, or the way I should do my hair, and lately she's even tried to give me marital advice! It's embarrassing but I try to be patient because I think she's lonely and wants to make my life better but holy-schmoely, she's really *starting to get on my nerves.*

Signed,
Bugged

Dear Bugged,

I've always loved that scene in *The Deer Hunter* where Robert DeNiro tries to explain to an uncomprehending John Cazale that the bullet in his hand *really is* the bullet in his hand, and not something else. Sitting on the hood of that beat-up Cadillac, he holds the bullet up, points to it and angrily declares:

> *"This is this. This ain't something else.* This *is* this."

There are lots of ways to talk about the problem of denial, but his is certainly one of my favorites. It speaks to the uncomfortable first step we must take as slayers, where we admit to ourselves that our vampires really *are vampires,* and *not* something else.

That intruding and advice-giving neighbor who can never take a hint to leave is not "just lonely and trying to help." She's a vampire, and she's feeding on me.

That isolating and critical spouse who is never satisfied no matter what I do is not "just a loner and telling it like it is." He's a vampire, and he's feeding on me.

Denial really is our vampires' best friend, which means my advice to you, sweetheart, since you're asking, is to wake up and smell the vampire.

PVS

....

6

Living in Darkness

Denial and the Birth of the Vampire

THAT GRAND OLD WATCHER VAN HELSING HIMSELF once warned us that: "*The strength of the vampire is that people will not believe in him,*" and for my part, I think he was right. Denial is a miraculously powerful ally to our vampires, because, let's face it, there's nothing like having a host look the other way to give a vampire free rein over their lives.

There are two main categories of denial that we practice most often. They are

1. our flat-out refusal to acknowledge the presence of a vampire when it's feeding on us, even when it's dangling from our necks for all to see;
2. our stubborn insistence that—even if it is a vampire hanging there by its fangs—it's really not as bad as it looks.

Let's begin with that first category: this remarkable ability we have to look a vampire straight in the eye and still not see it. Van Helsing was right: our denial is the vampire's greatest strength, but that's not all it is. I believe it is also a great source of comfort to our vampires—this ability we have to deny not only their existence, but also the existence of practically anything else we don't want to see. All that exercise in denial, and this training we do as we push aside first this fact and then the other, keeps us fit and ready, so when the moment arrives for us to deny any evidence of the vampires in our lives, we're in near-Olympic shape to handle it.

Thanks to lifetimes of dedicated training and practice, it's almost never too early in the day for us to dispose of any fact that we'd just as soon do without.

Here are a few examples of the kinds of things we deny that occur in the first . . . oh, maybe 90 minutes of an average workday:

- Denial of the fact that it really *is* time to get up when the alarm clock goes off: we fall back to sleep and consequently have to rush to get ready—which in turn makes us bite the head off of anyone who happens to be using the stove (they were there first) while we're hurrying to get our coffee
- Denial of *any* fact our bathroom scale has to tell us about our weight—unless by some amazing chance it's actually something we want to hear
- Denial that the guy driving in front of us is not so much a slow driver as *we* are just very late for work and are simply perceiving him to be slow.
- Denial of the fact that when we pass him at 85 miles an hour, we are putting plenty of other people—children

we've never met and their parents included—in danger besides ourselves

But that's just the beginning, and these are, comparatively speaking, really only the "little" denials. Here are a few of the tougher, 24-hour-a-day type:

- The fact that our smoking is hurting not only us, but everyone around us—especially our kids
- The fact that if we don't start eating right and exercising, we really are going to feel rotten when we're older ... if we live that long
- The fact that we have alcoholism or other addictions that are stealing our lives—and our loved ones' too
- The fact that there is something *else*—something only we know about, a secret we've kept for years, perhaps—and it's eating us alive
- The fact that we continue to be in relationship with and feed partners, friends, employers, neighbors, and beliefs that are vampires to us, and the clock keeps ticking, meaning that if we don't get slaying here pretty soon, they're going to get away with stealing the rest of our lives, too

I mentioned the second category of denial earlier—the one where we acknowledge the presence of a vampire in our lives, but keep telling ourselves it's not really that bad—and this is one that scares me, because it does the kind of damage to us (and worse, to our loved ones) that's so easy to miss.

I'm talking about the little things I get furious about every day, like maybe the way my family throws all their stuff on the counter I just cleared off and made beautiful as soon as they walk through the door. Or it might be the friend I have who just assumes my time, my home, and even my belongings are theirs to use without asking. There's my daughter's messy room that I've told her a thousand times to clean before she leaves the house. Or it could be the beautiful—and by that I mean gorgeous—dinners I make about four nights a week that no one even bothers to come to the table on time to eat.

You know this stuff: it's so small and insignificant that we don't want to mention it and there's no need to bother, right? The stuff that's not so bad. Can you think of one that gets you every day? Because now I'd like to point out the dangers of swallowing these resentments back.

To begin with, I keep them secret. I refuse to explain to anyone why these little things they do drive me nuts, and when I don't scream or even talk about what's bothering me, then I inevitably scream or talk about what's *not* bothering me instead. I begin *misrepresenting* myself, which

1. makes the people around me think I'm crazy, because the stuff I end up screaming and complaining about is usually NOTHING, and;
2. makes people around me try to help fix all the wrong stuff so I won't get upset. After all, when I'm mad about the dinner but complain about how annoying the show on TV is, all my loved ones learn to do is turn the TV off when I'm around.
3. Then there's the problem of people not even knowing who I really am because I keep denying the truth about my thoughts and feelings. Plus;
4. I hurt everybody's feelings by being such an unpredictable grouch—which serves no good purpose anyway, since;

5. it does nothing to get rid of the vampires that are making me crazy in the first place.

There are many perfectly appropriate and useful times for us to employ our aptitude for denial, especially since we all have experiences that we cannot and should not absorb fully or immediately. But these little things? These will do better out in the light, where they make at least a little more sense, and where everyone can see them.

How Vampires Benefit from Our Denial

You may or may not know this, but a vampire's nighttime vision is 20/20. That's not exactly as much a mythological "rule" as it is a "fact," and one we want to keep in mind for a couple of very good reasons.

The first and most important is that when we try to deny things about ourselves that we might be ashamed of by pushing them away and into the dark, we may not be able to see them, but our vampires surely can. So if we're trying to deny any less-than-noble inclinations we might have, like dishonesty or greed or pettiness—or the things we are ashamed of, like inattention to our health, our addictions, any other secrets we're holding on to—and pushing those things in the dark where we don't have to look at them, just remember: our vampires can see them with perfect clarity, even if we can't. So if, for instance, we refuse to see the truth about an addiction we have, our vampires—being able to see clearly where we've shoved the truth into the dark—can use that thing we're addicted to in such a way as to manipulate or control us. And we wonder how they can possibly know our secrets and precisely how to hurt us!

The second reason is a bit more obvious, and it's simply that we're not designed to see well in the dark, which makes it just about the worst place we can go rushing off to without light and a really good plan. Moral here: We never attempt to slay, revoke an invitation to, or even confront a vampire when we're upset and unprepared, because it means we're acting on impulse, and sure to wind up in a bad neighborhood.

Unfortunately, this is exactly what so many of us do: we go running headlong into the dark when we're angry, fooling ourselves into thinking our anger will protect us and give us power—which *it will not*. Running this way is one of the most efficient ways for us to get lost and end up in trouble with our vampires. By bolting after our vampires in a rage and ending up in their part of town, into their "Mother Night," they're able to watch us from shadowy corners, filing their nails and making note of our weaknesses.

Another advantage they gain by our denial is the time they buy. Just like heroes in any other vampire story, we too can waste a lot of time hoping these monsters turn out to be something—anything—other than what they really are. Just like in the movies, as the heroes watch people around them either die or become vampires and still insist there must be another explanation, we too, insist that our vampires cannot be real: that our coughs are from colds and not smoking; that our fatigue and tight clothes are not lack of exercise and overeating, but a temporary condition from which we will magically bounce back. We too insist that our abuser is not cruel but only misunderstood, and that our secrets will hurt us more if they are let out than they will if we keep them hidden. We'll do anything to keep from calling our vampires by their true names and seeing them for what they really are. As if denying the truth will change it.

My alcoholism was a lot like that: it was a disease I needed help with, but I didn't want to call it that. What I did want to call it, though, was practically anything else. A mental illness? All-righty. A nutritional imbalance? Okay with me. A weak will? If you say so. How about a shortage of spirituality or a lack of self-knowledge? Fine and dandy.

As far as I was concerned, you could call it whatever you wanted, just as long as you didn't call it what it really was: a disease that I did not have the power to treat by myself, any more than I would have had the power to treat cancer or diabetes by myself. I was so wholly enthralled by my alcoholism that I could only admit the truth to myself after I'd gotten so sick and utterly lost that I couldn't muster up even one more ounce of denial about it. It wasn't until I was that exhausted, with no cards left to play, that I was finally ready to admit to the deepest and stillest part of myself, "I give up: I know I can't beat it alone and I'm done trying to keep it in my life by pretending it's something else that I will someday magically fix. I don't know what I'm going to do about it yet—all I know is I'm done."

On the other hand, I think that if I'd had even the tiniest bit of fight left in me at all, I'd have kept right on swinging—and do you want to know why?

Because it's so much easier to do that than to admit something as frightening as our own vampire really does exist.

When I admit I'm in the thrall of a vampire, it means I'm also admitting they exist exactly as they are, and not as something else. They're not something that's easier for me to handle or that I might still be able to manage somehow. And this is where it gets personal, because the truth is that you've got your vampires and I've got mine, and one of the things that define them as vampires for us personally is the fact that *we cannot manage them*.

Alcohol might not be a vampire to you—to you it might be something you can manage and never thought twice about in your life—but to me, it's a vampire, and for me to admit my relationship with it is exactly as it is and not something else is admitting that I cannot manage it.

Let's say for you, though, the vampire is a shopping addiction or an abusive spouse. One way you can identify it as a problem is by noticing how much energy you put into denying the fact that it's hurting you and how hard you fight to maintain control of it so that you can keep it in your life—even though it's tearing your life apart. That's a pretty strong clue that you're dealing with a vampire: when it's hurting you that badly and you fight as hard as you can to keep it in your life anyway. And let me tell you, if it were an allergy to strawberries we were talking about that was ruining your life, I bet you'd have no trouble at all admitting that you couldn't manage the effect they had on you and revoke your invitation to them, would you? But a vampire is something we fight to keep. And how do we fight to keep it? With denial, that's how.

There are lots of things I can manage in this life, but managing something that's a vampire to me? Not only can't I manage it, I can't even stop myself from continuing to *try* managing it. I can't evict it without light or without help. I can't get rid of it alone, and as hard as I've tried to teach myself how to control it in the dark where no one else can see me, I just can't do it. I have to come into the light. I have to have help.

The trouble with getting help out of our vampire's thrall is that it usually means having to do things we're not that crazy about the prospect of doing, and taking steps we're not that hot on the prospect of taking. It usually means we're going to have to live by some rules that we never had anything to do with creating, that we're going to have to take some medicine we never wanted to take. Worst of all, we're going to have to face some fears about living *without* our vampires we never wanted to face.

No matter how awful our vampires are, sometimes the vampire we know can still seem easier to deal with than a future we don't.

That's what I think I'm doing when I deny all my other vampires, too: that I'm somehow saving myself the trouble (and the terror) of facing the truth and all of its unknown consequences. Although I can certainly see why it might seem easier to do that, I also think it's worth stopping to analyze for just a second.

Think about it: Where does the truth go when we deny it, anyway? Does it simply clear out of the way and never bother us again?

I guess it might be nice to pretend that the truth goes quietly away like that—that it bends meekly to our will and disappears into the dark forever. But personally, I don't think the truth takes rejection any better than I do.

Rejection doesn't feel very good. You've probably been given the opportunity to find that out at some point in your life. I know I have. I've had enough experience with being ignored, dismissed, and pushed aside to know my usual response to it, and I'll tell you what: I may be an inconsolable puddle of slop for a little while, but sooner or later, I start to get mad. My forehead starts to wrinkle, my fingers tense into little hooks, my nails get all long and dirty, and before I know what's happening, these fangs come slipping out from under my upper lip.

Dracula at the helm. Vampire in charge.

I think that the well-intentioned facts about our lives we choose to deny or reject respond in exactly the same way; they become vampires whose thirst for revenge is unquenchable. They feed on the living and their need for acknowledgment never dies—which, I suppose, is why we call them "undead" in the first place.

I believe when we deny the compassionate and well-meaning truth—despite our best efforts to kill it—it remains undead and becomes in a sense *reborn*, often as an unrelenting and merciless vampire who will do anything, apparently, to get our attention.

Vampires don't come out of nowhere. They only seem to, which is one of the things that make their appearance in our lives so frightening. Often when they show up, it feels like a surprise attack or ambush ... although, as creatures of the night they can hardly help coming at us from the dark. I mean, when you think about it, how much choice do they really have?

And not to be, like, overly sympathetic with them or anything, I have to say that that I don't think all vampires are necessarily "born bad," either. Not most of them, anyway.

The Birth of the Vampire

It's like in the movie *Bram Stoker's Dracula*. In the beginning, they show us that Dracula wasn't always a vampire. He didn't come out of the womb that way. No indeed.

As the story opens, we see that he was once a young Romanian knight, on his way to war against the Muslim Turks. At first sight, he is a handsome young soldier bidding a passionate farewell to his enchanting wife, Elizabeta—whom, our narrator tells us, he prizes above all things. As they say their goodbyes, we are warned that he might never return.

That's war for you.

Next scene: The battlefield, where the director shows us what might be just a bit more than we care to see of Dracula's fairly repulsive victory over the Turks. There's lots of vivid (and perhaps unnecessary) impaling going on in this scene, along with lots of bloodcurdling (and *surely* necessary) cries of anguish to go along with it.

When the battle ends and Dracula has won, he falls to his knees and thanks God for his victory. Then, sensing the call of beloved Elizabeta, he begins the long journey back home. But...

The Turks prove themselves to be both sore and clever losers: intent on winning a brutal game of *gotcha last*, they send a false message to Elizabeta which claims Dracula has died in battle, and, predictably overwhelmed by her grief, she dives from the castle window and to her death in the river below.

Score one for the Turks.

As Dracula enters the castle, he discovers his beautiful young wife lying dead at the foot of an altar. A suicide note lays on her chest, explaining how she—unable to bear her separation from him in this life—has killed herself in order to meet with him in the next. Also on the scene, however, is a small group of clerics, one of whom offers Dracula what is doubtless the most appallingly ill-timed piece of intelligence I've ever heard. He tells Dracula—if you can believe it—that there's no way he'll be meeting Elizabeta in heaven, since she has committed suicide and is therefore damned to hell.

Honestly. He couldn't put a hold on that news for just one minute? Poor Dracula is now so enraged that he looks to the heavens, renounces God, promises to rise from his own death to avenge Elizabeta's, and then vows to use all the powers of darkness to do it, too. It's a real mess.

But there's a moral to this story, and here it is:

To create a vampire, all you need do is
separate a person from love.

The Turks knew it. They knew, if you really want to hurt a guy, you can forget about knives, swords, and impaling sticks. They knew that if you *really* want to destroy someone, all you need to do is take away the thing they love most—the thing that helps them make sense of their lives. You take away the power that moves them from one task to the next: you take away their love.

It's so simple because when you remove love from somebody's life, you present that person with the best reason they will ever find to separate themselves from whatever God they depend on. When you take out the person or people they share their deepest love with, you've got a pretty good shot at tempting them to abandon their loving source of power altogether.

I once heard someone define hell as "a separation from God," and that made a lot of sense to me. I think it's possible for us to get so hurt, particularly if we lose what we love and cherish most, that we just sort of go: "Forget it; this life is just too painful for me now. The part of me that trusted the Big Picture or the Plan, the Higher Power or God, the Universe or the Creator—whatever you want to call it—is gone. I don't trust God and I don't trust life any more, either."

And then we *split*, so to speak.

The part of us that leaves our God naturally goes into the dark, all by itself, and plots its revenge. It is cold and alone and loveless, and wants nothing more than to go back where it is warm and populated and full of love, and really mess that place and its inhabitants up, but good. Just like the truth we send packing about our own vampires every time we deny their existence: whether that truth is about our weight problems, our marriage problems, our addictions, or just some neighbor who's driving us nuts and we don't want to admit it. If it's the truth, it doesn't like to be separated from us or denied either. Just like us, it does not wish to be discarded—or even worse, abandoned—not by us or by God or by anyone else. Nothing wants to live in exile.

Vampires are born every day—every minute, in fact—and it doesn't just happen "out there." There are plenty of them born right inside of us: the parts of ourselves that get driven into the dark for telling us a truth we don't want to hear, or for pointing out a reality we cannot bear to see.

"Listen," we say, "I just can't deal with you at the moment. You are way more information than I can process, and I want you out of here. Now." And off that part of us goes, cast out into the darkness, to the Lair of the Undead.

Only that part of us doesn't die, of course. And since its death is both incomplete and premature, it is simply *not done*. It cannot stay buried nor can it survive in the light. Like a sulking and angry ghost, it lives neither here nor there.

No wonder we call them "the undead." And no wonder they keep looking for invitations to get back in. I have no doubt that they only wish to complete what they started and then die peacefully, just like the rest of us, once and for all.

Note to vampires: Help is on the way, fellas. We're coming to get you.

II

Biting Back

7

What We'll Need to Fight

The Slayer Arsenal

THERE IS A SET OF WEAPONS ESSENTIAL to all vampire encounters and with which all slayers must become adept. As we train ourselves to use these weapons and begin to comprehend their power and reliability, we will experience our first real taste of what it is to be a slayer. We will begin to detect an inner strength and surefootedness that we've long since forgotten or perhaps never even knew we possessed. With determination and practice, we will discover the cool and capable slayer within each of us—one from whom straightforward and precise revocations flow smoothly; one whose slayings are performed with confidence and resolve.

Here are the weapons:

- clarity
- humility
- light
- Watchers

Also, I think I'll just go ahead and say this right now: If there's anyone out there thinking of trying to go into battle *without* these weapons, I suggest they loosen their collars, lift their chins, and prepare for a nice, long, lingering drink from their vampires.

Successful vampire slayers don't just cross their fingers, go skipping off into the dark all by themselves, and hope to skewer their vampires with the first stick they can find. Slayers who mean business stay in the light. They know who, what, and where their vampires are, and arm themselves with meticulously carved stakes they've learned exactly how to use.

Slayers whose revocations are acknowledged and taken seriously don't go charging into their vampire's lair and hope they'll be able to improvise an effective revocation once they get there. They understand the importance of thoughtful composition and exact timing, and have been taught to meet their vampires with revocations that are honest, clear, and precise.

Awareness of what we're doing and why we're doing it is fundamental to practical vampire slaying. Unless we're ready to take an honest look at who we are and what we're willing to do to be free of our vampires, our efforts won't amount to much more than dress-up and playacting, swagger and pretense—fine for people who don't care how silly they look or ineffective they are, but preposterous for serious vampire slayers. For us, all that theatre is just another way of staying in the problem and in the dark. For us, the importance of getting out of that darkness and into the light cannot be overstated.

Rather than impulsively running into combat with our vampires, shaking our fists and saying a lot of things we'll doubtless be sorry for later on, we, as effective slayers, instead prepare for battle by calmly and respectfully asking ourselves

> *"Am I really through with this vampire, or am I just waving a stick around and making threats?"*

I've done so much of that in my life: threatening to give up the booze, threatening to give up the crummy relationships, threatening to give up the lousy eating habits, the crappy jobs. I've stomped out and slammed the door on that stuff a million times, I bet, only to come sneaking back in later to snuggle with the bottle, the guy, the food, the employer, whatever it was. Just the two of us, all cozy-schmozy—together again.

Sweet, but not very productive, right? The second all that sweetness wore off, all the same old fears, resentments, and problems would return, and there I'd be, right back where I'd started. All that door slamming and walking out never really changed anything for me, unless you want to count how it helped to wear me down in a kind of "straw-that-broke-the-camel's-back" sense. The sheer monotony and uselessness of those performances might have played a part in my *getting ready* to change—but as far as my actually *being* ready to change? That was something else.

One Road to Clarity

When I was thirty-seven years old and about six months into my recovery from alcoholism, I began to notice that much about my relationship with my boyfriend was no longer working as well as it once had. There was this way we'd learned to live together in the disease—an understanding we had about my inferiority to him as a drug addict and alcoholic, and his superiority to me as a ... well, neither one of those, I guess.

The person I'm speaking of is still one of the best friends I've ever had, but what we had in the end there was pretty much your standard contract for unhealthy relationships between alcoholics and codependents. One of us had to play the strong, responsible one and the other had to play the weak, irresponsible one, and that was my role. I don't think those roles were a conscious choice for either of us; they were just a natural outgrowth to my alcoholism and the two of us living with that disease. Anyone would have gotten as sick as we did, because that's how alcoholism works: it's just so fantastically toxic to everything it touches, even when nobody dies.

But then an odd thing happened. One day I stopped drinking. I didn't mean to, and it certainly wasn't part of any master plan I'd designed, but just the same, the moment came when I just couldn't make myself drink anymore. What seemed even worse to me at the time was that, try as I might, I couldn't quite make myself die, either. So I couldn't drink and I couldn't die, and that meant I had only one very bleak option left: the one I never wanted to face and was positive I'd never be able to handle, which was to somehow try and find a way to live the rest of my life without drugs or alcohol. You can imagine the impact this had on my relationship with my boyfriend.

A lot changes when you stop medicating your pain in the same old way you always have. For one thing, I had no more drug-induced vacations from all the hurt and anger that had been a big part of our relationship. That led to such a huge backlog of unalleviated sadness and resentment I didn't think I could hold inside anymore.

Also, I don't think either of us really knew how to act in our new roles. I certainly didn't know how to behave in a relationship as a clean and sober person with him, and my guess is that he didn't really know how to respond to me in that new condition, either. We were so entrenched in our old patterns of relating that we could barely be in the same room together without screaming at each other, and there was one thing I was reluctantly coming to understand about it: if I didn't find a new way to fix the pain I was experiencing, I would sooner or later fix it in the same old way I always had before.

I certainly didn't see my pain in that relationship as a vampire to me back then; that way of perceiving it came to me much later on. What I did finally come to see, though, was that the sadness we were causing each other no longer had a useful place in my life. I was done with that pain and willing to do whatever was necessary to end it, only now drinking and using weren't options for making it go away. They didn't work.

There was one last argument we had together—our very last—and I can remember how in the middle of it and without any warning, I stopped fighting, because very suddenly, it seemed that I had absolutely nothing left to say. It wasn't like some big spiritual insight struck me or I had an epiphany that left me speechless, but it *did* feel like the thing that had driven me to scream and fight with him all those years was done. And when it was done I didn't have any more reason to slam the doors, stomp my feet, shriek, swear, or even speak. I was quiet all over, inside and out.

Sometimes I think the reason it got so still and quiet within me like that was because I was so full that nothing inside of me could move. I don't think I had room for one more drop of arguing or negotiating; the last drop of that had filled whatever space inside me had held it all, and that was the end of it. I remember having a very *physical* feeling of fullness, and when a cup is full there's really no point in arguing about whether it can hold any more or not. It just can't, and it's ridiculous to argue: the thing is done.

That's the long and dark road to clarity for me, the one that brought me, after trying as hard as I could to keep what had become a very painful relationship in my life, to finally seeing that I just couldn't do it. I had neither the capacity to keep the vampire in my life nor the strength to deny its presence. I was full and empty at the same time; and was done fighting. All that was left was the truth, quiet and still.

Humility

There's a bonus hidden in traveling on dark roads. At the end of them and in that moment of clarity, we also begin to receive the gift of humility—by which I mean that we begin to know the truth about ourselves. Nothing more or less than that. That's all humility is: knowing the simple truth about ourselves, and my experience with it is very much like living in a dark room for many years and then having the light come on.

I'd love to be able to say how that light is pure white and full of love and all that—and there are times when it *is* kind of lovely. But there have also been times when the experience has been fairly grim, and it's more like having the light come on in a basement that I didn't know I'd been living in for years, and then looking around and realizing there are boxes of stuff all over the place that I haven't used or even looked into for so long—even though I've been navigating around and tripping over them all that time.

Sometimes when the light comes on we see that the room we've been living in is pretty gray, and other times it comes on and we see how beautiful it is and how fortunate we've been. But light is just light: all it can do is illuminate the truth of what's really there. And while truth is always with us, it can also get buried in the darkness of our fear, denial, or pride—hiding where we can't see it. The longer it stays hidden, the more frightening the prospect of seeing it becomes to us, and we come to fear it as if it were Medusa herself. We'll turn to stone if we dare look at it.

It's not the truth or humility that hurts us so much, though. It's our reluctance about uncovering truth after it's been hidden so long that smarts. I'm sure the uncovering is why humility has such a terrible reputation. We mistake it for the pain we experience trying to *avoid* it. We mistake it for the pain we get when we're trying to make something work in our lives that just cannot work anymore—like me with my drinking or with my old boyfriend. There was a time when each of those things worked for me, and a time when they didn't anymore, and what hurt so much was not that they'd stopped working, but rather that I kept trying to force them to. All that pushing is so tiring and discouraging, and can become yet another vampire to us—a vampire of despair that makes staying in the dark start to look like a pretty good idea, as it whispers to us that returning to the light would be too hard and that we probably don't really belong there.

But it lies.

While I realize this may be obvious to you, I'm going to say it anyway: the fact that certain things in my life stop working for me almost never means those things are "bad" in themselves*, especially when we're talking about things like alcohol or relationships we have with perfectly fine and wonderful people—these are obviously not bad things. They're just examples of things that some of us develop a kind of allergy to and *become* vampires to us, probably because when they stopped working for us we refused to see the truth of that and change the way we related to them. It's just like that whole denial thing we were talking about earlier: we push the truth into the dark where it turns into a vampire, and then by the time we let it out it's lost its manners. It can be pretty hurtful and seem bad ... but really, it's just the truth, returning to the light and still feeling a little sore at us about keeping it in the dark so long.

Taking that road is fairly fundamental to being human and to growing up, I think. If we're lucky enough to mature at all in our lives, it will be because we've learned to face the truth about

---

*Although I must emphasize that some vampires really *are* bad in themselves; some people and things are just bad for us, no matter what, and don't you forget it.

ourselves. And if we're really lucky, we'll eventually be so humbled by the sheer power of that truth that we might even come to desire humility as a necessary ingredient to living a sane and contented life.

Or at least I did. Do. And although the long road is a perfectly good one, I have since learned there's a shorter road available to us—quicker and a lot less painful—if we want to take it.

A Second Road to Clarity: Bringing the Light with Us

My dear friend and longtime Watcher Julie taught me about this shorter road to finding clarity, humility, and the plain old truth about ourselves—but the catch to it is this: before we can know the truth about ourselves, we have to *want* to know that truth first. And that might entail a few consequences we haven't yet considered.

For starters, it could mean finding out you're not exactly the person you've always liked to think you are. Or that some of the secrets you've been keeping about what you've been up to are going to have to come into the light where you can see them—which could also mean you'll end up needing to make some honest and unselfish decisions about them.

It could mean discovering you're not nearly as innocent or secure or even sane as you thought you were. Worse, it could mean finding out you're not even as plain old *nice* as you might once have liked to think, either.

Because nice guys don't evict their vampires, right? Nice guys don't tell their vampires they want them to leave—nice guys just politely wait around for their vampires to leave without having to be asked. Nice guys don't tell their vampires what it is they want or don't want from them. Nice guys just drop about a thousand hints per minute, hoping their vampires will finally take one of them and start behaving themselves. Nice guys don't meet their vampires face-to-face in the light and speak honestly to them about how they feel. Nice guys just gossip about what jerks their vampires are behind their backs and then make themselves sick with resentment when their gossip hasn't changed the fact that their vampires are still jerks. Nice guys don't admit they have neither the strength nor the desire to keep feeding their vampires anymore. Nice guys would rather suffer before an audience of sympathetic friends and family while their vampires bleed them of everything they've got, leaving them with nothing to give their friends or families because they've given every last bit of it to their vampires. Because they're so nice.

Pride is surely part of what makes it so hard for us to want to know the truth about ourselves. But there's something else more subtle and indirect than pride: it's that inability so many of us have to "stay present" in our lives, to keep our hands and our minds in the same place at the same time. It's easy to get lost in the past and the future, to get so preoccupied with our worries, regrets, and expectations that we don't even know where we are or what we're doing half the time, and that's no way to live in the light where we can see what's going on.

The method we'll be using to find our truth involves letting go of all that past and future thinking, and spending some time alone and quiet, all by ourselves and on purpose.

I'll say that again: *On purpose*. If we're going to know the truth about ourselves, we have to *want* to know it first. Self-knowledge doesn't just happen by accident: it takes desire, willingness, and discipline—which is something a lot of us really hate to even think about. Just like wanting to have a clean kitchen, clean teeth, and/or physical strength, we have to discipline ourselves to get them.

Before Julie could teach me this shortcut method, though, she first had to teach me one of the most important distinctions I'll ever learn in my life: the distinction between saying "I *can't* do thus-and-such," and saying, "I *don't want* to do thus-and-such."

For some time after that moment of clarity I had when I saw I was done fighting with my boyfriend and left, the two of us still saw each other occasionally, and were still discussing whether we should try to get back together again or not.

Please understand that even though I'd had a moment of clarity, I was still filled with doubts about my ability to end the relationship entirely, and this is a very important thing to be aware of, since so many of us—even after seeing the truth about ourselves and our vampires—still struggle with the logistics of such realizations. *Seeing* the vampire is not *slaying* the vampire, remember? Just like the slayers in *'Salem's Lot* after they found where the vampires were hiding, I too still had a lot more work to do. Just because we've recognized a vampire does not mean we have a plan for living without it yet.

It was on a beautiful autumn afternoon that I was having one of those discussions with my almost-ex. We were talking outside my house and Julie was inside, with the front door open. She knew all about how we'd been struggling with our breakup, of course, and after he left and I came into the house, she was waiting there for me.

She said, "I'm sorry, Claud, but I couldn't help overhearing your conversation out there and you know what? I think I've figured out why you guys keep having the same conversation over and over again. I think I've figured out why he can't hear you."

I imagined she was going to say something to cheer me up about what a gentle, lovely person I was and what a fascist bully he was but she didn't.

Instead, she said, "The reason he can't hear you is that you're not giving him the information he needs to understand you. You're not telling him the truth."

I was shocked. This was *my* fault? "What do you mean?" I asked her.

"The problem is," she said, with a tiny grin, "that you're telling him you *can't* be with him."

"Yeah, and I can't," I said, starting to get a little irritated. "So what's the problem?"

"The problem is that when you tell him that you can't be with him, what he hears is that you *would* be with him if you *could*. When you tell a person who doesn't want to hear you say no that you can't do what they want you to do, they automatically assume that you *want* to say yes, but that something is standing in your way so you can't. Their job, they think, is to determine what that thing is that's in your way, and then move it out of the way. They want to fix it for you."

I thought about that for a minute. I thought about all the people I'd ever tried to politely avoid and all the ways they'd "fixed it" when I said I couldn't do whatever it was they wanted me to do, and while I saw what she meant, I still didn't see how I was going to get out of it. It seemed like... I don't know: some impossible-to-solve equation or something. But because she was such a fabulous Watcher and always had the greatest solutions to problems I couldn't even begin to solve, I asked her anyway. I said, "So what can I do?"

"Well," she said, "I think you can start by knowing the answer to that question yourself... what is your answer, anyway? If you *could* be with him, *would* you be with him?"

It was a distinction I'd never even considered. I'd been making it sound like my hands were tied and I had no say in the matter. I'd been making it sound like there was a vampire in my house; like I had nothing at all to do with inviting him in.

"Not today," I said, finally. "I wouldn't want to be with him today, even if I could be ... but I don't know about tomorrow." I paused, "Is that an okay answer?"

She nodded her head, "Yep. And I think I see the missing piece: The reason you can't tell him what you want is because you don't even know what that is yourself. How can you possibly expect to be clear with him when you're not even clear with yourself yet?"

"Yeah," I said, trying to imagine myself telling him that it was absolutely over, "but this is so hard. I don't want to hurt him."

"I know," she said kindly, "this stuff *is* really hard. But I think you owe it to yourself and to him, too, if you really care about his feelings, to take some time to get quiet with yourself and to, you know—ask yourself the question."

"Ask myself what question?"

"I'm not positive about this, but I think the question for you is something like: *What do I want and what am I willing to risk losing in order to get it?*

"And then," she said, "all you have to do is to wait and listen for the answer."

This was the shortcut I was looking for—a direct route to finding the truth about myself that I could take that I wouldn't practically have to die taking. It turned out to be so simple and so powerful, though, that I think I'd better issue this warning before I tell you how it's done.

If you've got a question about yourself that you really want an answer to, then look out, because you've already got it. Your answer is already there, waiting right inside you. This process is just like using that little flashlight icon that appears when you conduct a search on your computer: asking your question sets in motion the search for information that's already there—and since all you need to see it is light, once you press that search button, *you're going to find it.*

Your Spiritual Searchlight

Now some people might call this meditation, and maybe it is, but I see it more as a simple procedure for looking inside to find answers only you can provide. True, it certainly resembles the *spirit* of many meditations I've done, but I have to say that this particular process is pretty streamlined and singular in its purpose: you proceed with the specific intention of finding the truth on one very narrow and particular subject at a time.

As always when you want to concentrate, find a place where you can be alone to listen, and do whatever it takes to get it: lock the door, take the phone off the hook, and explain to your spouse, housemates, children, potential visitors, or pets, in friendly but luminously clear terms, you want to be left alone for a while. Then you find your notebook and pen, and go to your comfortable spot where you won't be disturbed. Sit down, quiet yourself, and think for a moment about why you are here. When you are composed and ready:

1. Take a deep and cleansing breath, and let it out.
2. Ask the God of your understanding to help and guide you, and then sit quietly until you are conscious of our God's attendance (God is always in attendance, of course; this is just a matter of becoming *conscious* of it—kind of like saying, "Hello," when you pick up a phone indicates that we want to talk and are ready to listen—but the connection, obviously, is already open) and you've made it clear to God that you've come for answers and you're listening carefully. Then, when you are focused and calm, you begin.

3. Ask "the question," that my Watcher told me (and which we'll refer to from now on as "the template question"):

"What do I want, and what am I willing to risk losing in order to get it?"

Write that question on the top page of your notebook, because it's your question, too. What you're doing here is asking for God's light and guidance to come and help you see the answer that's already in your heart. What you want to know by the time you're done is whether this is a vampire you want to do something about or not. If you do, then what are you willing to do or to lose in order to make that change happen?

In the case with my boyfriend, the template question as applied to my particular situation was, *"Do I want to be with him—and if I don't, then what am I willing to risk letting go of to be free of him?"*

Remember when we talked about the things we might see in ourselves that could surprise us? This is where that part came in for me, because in my case I saw a lot. When I asked the question "Do I want to be with him?" and the answer was no, an absolutely unstoppable flood of information about myself came pouring in for me to see. I saw fears I had about not being able to take care of myself (financial fears), fears about having to redefine myself without him (social insecurity and self-esteem issues), fears about what other people would think (doubts about my ability to make my own decisions), and especially fears about what would happen to me if I made a mistake and were left all alone with no love while the rest of the world said, "We told you so," for the rest of my life. It wasn't the greatest stuff to have to see in myself, but I'll say this for it: at least I knew what I was up against, who I was, and what I feared I had to lose if I left him. The lights were on and I had all the information I needed to make my decision.

But that was my experience, and now it's your turn.

It's time to go back to the steps. Begin by picking up that notebook, and **write this down** so you can see your thoughts in black and white, and watch their progression:

4. Let's say that in your case it's a job that has become a vampire to you and you haven't decided whether you want to do anything about it or not: you've seen the vampire, but now it's just lying there, under the porch like it was for those *'Salem's Lot* slayers. Applying the template question to your own situation, you would ask: *"Do I want to leave my job, and if I do, then what am I willing to risk losing or let go of to be free of it?"*
5. Let's assume that your answer here is "YES! I'd love to leave that job!" but... then your fears start showing up. They tell you that you might not be able to get another job, you're too old, not well-educated enough, not good-looking enough anymore to compete, that your spouse or partner will be unhappy with you, and that you'll make a wrong decision that will land you and your family in cardboard boxes living under a bridge somewhere. While any or all of your fears may seem silly or exaggerated, whatever they are, if you've got them, *write them down*: these are your thoughts and you want to keep track of them. This is you with the light on in the basement, looking at those unopened boxes you've been tripping over all these years—and it's a good, really good, thing.
6. Next, since you've still not come to a peaceful conclusion, you have more to do. Your next question would be:

   "What is the very bottom line for me? What is the one or at the very most two things that must change in order for this job to stop being a vampire to me?"

Then start writing. What is it that will bring you peace? Is it more praise or verbal recognition for all your hard work that will do it? Is it a raise of 15 percent per year? Is it a longer lunch hour? Better training? Your own office? What's your bottom line?

7. When you know your bottom line, *ask yourself what you're willing to risk losing or letting go of to have it.* Are you willing to risk losing your job for it? Are you willing to let go of your fear of not getting another job if you give your employer an ultimatum? Are you willing to have your spouse or partner snarl at you for a while? Whatever your answers are, keep this in mind: this is your bottom line, which means that unless you take some kind of action on it, nothing will change and the days you've been spending at work miserable will continue to be days that you spend at work miserable. Remember, you're done with denial and in the light now, and the fact is that *if you don't change this, it won't get changed.*
8. This is the process you use until you come to peace with your answer. And here's the good news: even if you do, in the end, decide that you're more comfortable doing nothing for now and making no changes whatsoever, you've still taken an action that will alter your relationship—not with your employer—but with yourself and your *inner* vampire. You've brought light into your heart, you've stopped hiding and have now considered the truth about your vampire, yourself, your options, and what's more, you've taken responsibility for them. At the very least (and it's plenty!) your days of seeing yourself as a victim are over. You know what you're doing and why you're doing it; you've made a choice that no vampire is "forcing" you to make. And you know what? That makes you free.

I like to remind myself of that point when I'm angry with someone about something I haven't bothered to address with them, and find myself stewing on it again. I think, "You've considered your options and decided of your own free will not to take action—and Claudia, you can hardly consider yourself a victim if you haven't even given them a chance to know what's bothering you and to change it!" Every time I remind myself of those facts, it quiets my rage; every time I do that, I stop being a victim in my own mind.

Peace.

As long as we've gone through the process, then we can always remind ourselves, the next time we're about to get mad about our vampire, that it was *our choice* not to take action. We've considered our options and chosen of our own free will to do nothing about it, at least for today. No victim = no vampire. And plus, you know what? We can always re-evaluate our vampire and how we feel about it any time we want to: the freedom to consider our options and take action never goes away; it's always ours.

Because those are the rules, too.

More Light, More Clarity, More Humility: Ours for the Receiving

There is one addition or even substitution you can make in this high-speed process of coming to the truth about your vampire and yourself, and that one addition is to enlist the help of a Watcher. There's more than one way to bring light to a subject, and for some, and even many of us, an honest discussion with our Watcher is a helpful addition to or substitution for a quiet consultation with our God.

Finding Your Watcher

By now you probably have a pretty good idea of what a Watcher is, but since you've now come to thinking seriously about finding a good one for yourself (or two or three!), I'd like to go over a few of the qualities you should be looking for in yours:

- Your Watcher is someone who has experience with the path you are on and the vampire you're slaying. If your vampire is an obnoxious neighbor, your Watcher might be someone who has experience handling difficult neighbors successfully. If your vampire is a difficult employer or spouse, you look for a Watcher who is happy in her/his job or marriage, and has dealt successfully with problems in both. If your vampire is an addiction, you find someone who has experienced the same addiction you have and succeeded in becoming free of it.
- Your Watcher should be someone who knows how to keep his/her mouth shut. They understand the importance of privacy, and *you* understand the importance of seeking out a Watcher whom you've never seen gossip or share another's personal problems with anyone else. Your Watcher is someone you have to be able to trust, and you can learn a lot by watching the way they behave when others in the room are gossiping: if they say nothing, change the subject, leave the room, or—as my Watcher Julie once did—tell the group that's gossiping that she'd like to stay but if they're going to gossip she'll have to leave—well, then you've found a Watcher who knows how to respect your privacy, too.
- Your Watcher has qualities that you'd like to have yourself. If you're not great at socializing but would like to be, you might keep your eye out for someone who is

comfortable that way. If you wish you were more open-minded, wished you laughed more than you do, wished you were more articulate, a better mechanic or cook—look for a Watcher who has qualities you'd like to develop in yourself.

- Your Watcher should never be a person who wants to play analyst with you, make judgments about you, or tell you what you should do. A good Watcher reflects and helps bring light and understanding to our problems—he/she never tells us what is wrong with us, what we should change, or rushes us into doing anything. They share their experience and what worked for them without expecting us to follow the exact same path that they did. This is why our clergy or best friend might not be the best person for the job: they may have an agenda or way of seeing things that makes them want to influence our perceptions and decisions. And some best friends—not all—are, like you, just too close to the problem to see it clearly.

I've heard it said so often that people hear God speak to them through other people, and that may be why bringing our Watchers along on our search for clarity works so well for many of us. For me, it's an addition, and a necessary one, almost every time—because I find that the extra dose of good intention and light they bring to the question keeps me honest. It's so easy to fudge when I'm alone. In fact, it's pretty easy to fudge with most people, but with my Watchers? I find it very difficult to lie or tell an incomplete truth (if there is such a thing!) to my Watchers. That's the way it works for me, but for some slayers, spending time with their Watchers in the pursuit of truth is actually their *only* way of consulting with their God, and so each of us does as our conscience directs and what works best for us. Besides, the procedure used in this search for clarity is similar to the last one I discussed—the addition of our Watcher being the only real difference.

For Slayers Who Choose to Do Their Search with a Watcher

As always, make sure you have a place where you can concentrate and won't be disturbed. Perhaps you have prepared for your meeting by writing a few ideas you already have about this vampire down in your notebooks. Bring those along to share with your Watcher, too.

Don't forget any coffee, tea, Mallomars, Kleenex, and/or ashtrays you might need, and then sit down and make yourselves comfortable. Quiet yourselves—perhaps beginning with a prayer or a few minutes of meditation to remember why you are there and what you are intending to accomplish. When you are composed and ready, you can begin:

1. Describe the situation to your Watcher and the details of how this person, situation, or belief is a vampire to you. It is essential that you do your best to be completely honest and thorough. Tell them exactly what's bothering you—no matter how petty or silly it may seem—and describe how this vampire is affecting you internally. The more truth you tell, the better you'll feel.
2. Your Watcher may help both of you understand the problem better by asking questions about it that he/she needs clarification on. Your Watcher's need for more information will help you discover and bring light to areas that are in the dark, and in this way can be a bright, instruc-

tive, and supportive light to you. Once the vampire has been thoroughly discussed and revealed, you will then be ready to ask the "template question."

3. Ask yourself (and answer your Watcher): *"What do I want, and what am I willing to risk losing in order to get it?"* Again: what you're doing here is asking your Watcher's light, support, and guidance to help you see what is in your heart. They will help you break the question down and restate it until you get an answer, just as you did in quiet contemplation with the God of your understanding.

When, with the help of God and/or our Watcher, we have clarity about what we want and what we're willing to risk getting it, we are then ready to consider our options. Remember when we talked earlier about there being more than one way to skin a vampire? Well, now it's time to learn exactly what that means, what those options are, and how they're executed.

If this is starting to feel real to you—you want to know why? Because it *is*.

8

The Menu

Choosing How to Bite Back

Bringing the truth about our vampires and ourselves into the light where we can see it is a great start, but it doesn't mean we've considered our slaying options or decided what we're going to do yet. Now is the time for choice. Now that we are in the light and can see what we're dealing with and who we are, we are ready to make clear and informed decisions about our lives and how we want to live them.

To begin, let's not assume that just because we've finally figured out who our vampires are and that we want to do something about them means we're automatically obligated to revoke our invitations or to slay our vampires.

Always try to keep in mind that practical vampire slaying is about restoring our personal freedom, which is to say that it involves *responsibility* in a big way, but involves *obligation* in no way at all. None of us can be free without a willingness to take responsibility for ourselves, of course, but as far as that "obligation" stuff goes, well…

A Brief Lecture on No-Good, Toxic Judgments

Practical vampire slaying is about making informed, conscious, and therefore free choices about our lives; it is not about following someone else's script for about what is supposedly best for us. No one is allowed to push us into revoking our invitations or slaying our vampires, and no one who knows what's good for them will so much as raise an eyebrow in our direction should we decide to do neither and keep our vampires around instead.

Aside from being in extremely poor spiritual taste, judging what another person chooses to do about their vampire is simply not a thing that any of us can reasonably expect to get away with. Many of us have tried pronouncing judgment on others and discovered, too late, that the price for that is just a little out of our range.

I'm talking about this "judge not, lest ye be judged," business, specifically, and it's not an adage we take lightly: no matter how we try to bend the rules or get around them, we will always find it impossible to judge someone else without judging ourselves right along with them. And that's the thing we need to be concerned about, of course: this problem of judging ourselves. There are two things I can tell you about self-judgment:

1. It's poison.
2. It comes hardest when it's on the heels of a judgment we've made about somebody else.

I swear, the second I say something critical about another person, the ball gets rolling: I complain about the way the guy in front of me is driving, and within about two minutes I'm the one who almost causes an accident. I gossip about some stupid thing a guy says in a meeting, and the next day *I'm* the guy saying something stupid in meeting—and beating the crap out of myself for it, too.

If only our judgments came from outside us, based on some universally agreed upon or objective standard. Then we could separate ourselves from their venom. We could just say, "That guy's wrong and I'm not" ... but of course that's not how it works. Our judgments come from *inside* us, based on our experience and what we've been taught, so it's really kind of silly to imagine we can separate ourselves from them.

As a matter of fact, I think there's a pretty well known prayer that makes this same connection, one that speaks of "forgiving our trespasses as we forgive those who trespass against us," so it's not as if this connection is completely unheard of. I'm not the only one who's noticed how having harsh opinions about others can make a deep and lasting impression—not upon how we view *them,* but rather upon how we view ourselves. And why would we be designed to escape the measure of our own standards, anyway? What would be fair, or even reasonable, about that?

As enlightened vampire slayers, we avoid making judgments about others—especially how they choose to handle their own vampires. What we discover as we try to practice this principle is that when we stop making judgments about other people, we become almost magically immune to the judgments that other people make about us. It's very mysterious and very cool, and it's just one of those things no one believes until they try it themselves, I guess. Like homeopathy. Or Krispy Kremes.

Besides, if it's really freedom we're searching for, then the decisions we make about our vampires have to be our own—which means that well-intentioned friends and family, professional advisors, and our present cultural standards don't really have a lot to say about them.

I'm not, however, so idealistic as to think other people's opinions or the standards we're exposed to won't influence our decisions to some degree, because the chances are pretty good they will. We're probably going to want to please other people and we'll probably believe that by doing what they want us to that we *will* please them. I get that. I just want to point out that neither the people we're trying to please nor the standards we're trying to meet have to live with or without our vampires, but *we do*. These are *our* lives we're making decisions about, not theirs.

So. Now that we're as ready we'll ever be to make an unprejudiced decision about the future disposition of our vampires, let's consider our options. Right off the bat, I can think of four:

1. Forgiveness

If we've recognized a vampire in our life and decided, after searching our soul and weighing all the pros and cons, that we're still not through with them and want to keep them in our lives, then this is the option for us. If we have quietly contemplated this with our God and with our Watcher, searched our hearts and know the truth there is that we still love them too much to let them go, then this may be as far as we get.

Far enough!

Whether our vampire is a crummy marriage or a lousy job, whether it's smoking cigarettes, eating too much sugar, or something else we feel is harmful to us but know in our hearts that we're still not ready to live without, then we can choose the option of simply accepting our vampire, making peace with ourselves, and living with it. We can choose to forgive. First, though, I'd like to define what we mean by that.

Because it seems to me, especially when I'm watching TV or listening to those call-in radio shows where people talk to psychologists or priests and they're talking about forgiveness, that misunderstandings abound.

Guests of the show or callers-in are always saying things like, "My husband left me and the kids fourteen years ago, and I know I've forgiven him in my heart, but sometimes I still get angry, so I wonder if there's a part of it I haven't gotten over yet."

"A part of it?" I always wonder: "What do they mean, 'a *part* of it?'" Do they mean the part where they've actually *forgiven* the offense? Is that the "part" they're referring to?

Such talk confuses me, and usually about the best I can do to explain these odd things people say is to think that maybe they had a moment when they felt tenderness toward their vampire and perhaps they mistook that feeling of tenderness for forgiveness. Because if they're still thinking about how somebody or something hurt them fourteen years ago and getting mad about it, then I really doubt they've experienced anything like real forgiveness yet.

Forgiveness isn't a feeling or sentiment we have about a person or thing. Forgiveness is *acceptance* of that person or thing exactly as they are. When we accept them it doesn't mean that we like them or condone what they did; it doesn't mean we understand it or feel sorry for them; and it definitely doesn't mean that what they did "is okay with us now," either. All it means is that we've made peace with ourselves about the fact that what happened did happen. It means we've reached a point where we've stopped saying, "This shouldn't have been," and started saying, "This was." And if you want to forgive your vampire and want to be absolutely sure that you understand what we mean when we talk about forgiveness,

You Can Test Yourself

Think of a something terrible that someone has done to you that you're not sure you've ever forgiven:

- Maybe it's the way your parents raised you.
- Maybe it's an affair your spouse or partner had.
- Maybe it's money or something of value that a friend promised to, but never did, return.
- Or maybe it's a lie you were told that the liar never corrected.

Whatever it is, it should be something you're not sure you've let go of, and when you've got it, ask yourself this: When my anger rises, am I'm still telling myself:

- That my parents *shouldn't have* made those mistakes?
- That my spouse/partner *shouldn't have* had the affair?
- That my friend *shouldn't have* taken my money/belongings?
- That the person who lied to me *shouldn't have* lied?

Because if you're still telling yourself "it shouldn't have happened" you're not done. You've not accepted the fact that it *did* happen, and there can be no forgiveness until you do.

How Forgiveness Feels

There was a point in my life when I got really busy and nuts, and so for convenience's sake, started living, almost exclusively, on microwaved hot dogs. I know. It was bad, and I chided myself for it all the time. I was so embarrassed that I tried to not let people know about it, but one day I was talking to my Watcher Julie and the truth came out. I told her I was worried about my eating habits and trying to hide them because they had become so embarrassing. And I told her, too, that I knew what I was doing was very wrong and bad for my health.

She listened to me for a while, and then she surprised the heck out of me when, instead of agreeing with me about how delinquent I was and how I really had to get on the ball with my nutrition, she simply said that she was worried, not about my nutrition, but the fact that I was beating myself up so much about it. She told me she thought it was fine that I'd recognized a problem (*vampire*) in my life and that I was taking responsibility (*acknowledging my invitation*) for it, but what she really wanted me to sit up and take notice of was the fact that I was saying such mean things to myself about it. She called it "bringing out the whip."

She said I'd taken what could have been useful information (that I could be taking better care of my health) and turned it into a whip (saying mean things to myself) to use against myself. She said it was a thing that happened a lot to people when they were trying to improve themselves. They would take what might have been a good thing—like wanting to exercise or eat right—and turn it into a whip they used to hurt themselves. If they failed, then they would tell themselves that they were lazy or fat or ridiculous, just as I'd been doing, and then beat themselves mercilessly with that whip every chance they got.

It's kind of like keeping a vampire around and beating ourselves up for it, too. More bargain basement vampires: two for the price of one.

She said: "You know what, Claud? I think that maybe, just for today, you're just going to have to be a person who eats hot dogs every day. I think you're going to have to accept that's just who you are for today. You're going to have to put down the whip and just know that about yourself and live with it.

"What do you think?" she asked, "Does that sound like something you might be able to do?"

And incredibly enough, it was. Suddenly it seemed like there was no more point in saying what I was *supposed* to be doing or what *should* have been, and that the truth was simply what it was: That I was a person who ate hot dogs all the time, and almost nothing else.

I was so happy after that—eating hot dogs without having to be so mean to myself about it! And I think it was the first time I'd ever experienced the way forgiveness and acceptance really feel: like embracing the truth, just as it is.

If you want to forgive your vampire and keep it around, I think it's a fine idea. Because maybe, just for today, you're a person whose parents did a rotten job raising them—and maybe for today that's as good as it's going to get. Maybe you're a person whose spouse cheated on them, whose friend ripped them off; maybe you're a person who's been lied to but never apologized to, and maybe—just for today—that's okay. Maybe that's just the way it is, and it's just going to have to be good enough.

As far as I'm concerned, whether it's hot dogs or a lousy job, it's absolutely fine to keep a vampire around. We all do it, or at least all the *best* people do. I'm pretty sure I don't have any friends who aren't thrashing around with at least one or two of their pet vampires every day, and it's not because they don't know how to revoke their invitations, either. They know exactly how to get rid of their vampires, only for now, they're simply choosing not to.

For now, they choose to live with their vampires. They choose to know it, and choose to forgive themselves and their vampires for it, too. For today, they say, "I live with a vampire. For today, this is who I am: a person who lives with a vampire." Can you imagine the freedom in that?

Having choice is a wonderful thing. It's way more than we had before we recognized our vampires and accepted responsibility for our invitations. At least we're no longer playing the unconscious victim in a horror show we have a feeling that somebody else is writing. We have chosen instead to be alert and responsible authors of our own scripts; what used to look like a horror show is now in the light where we can see it, and we're no longer afraid.

Plus, we can opt to rewrite the ending at any time. We can always change our minds if we want to. Isn't that excellent?

And that, as it happens, brings us to Option Number Two.

2. Wait and See

This is a good option for those of us who haven't yet had an epiphany about our vampire and perhaps never will, and also for those of us who, when we got quiet and asked for an answer about whether we wanted to keep our vampires around or not, didn't get a clear one. Of course there are times when our answers don't come right away, and of course there are times when we're just not ready to hear those answers right away, too. It doesn't mean those answers aren't in there and won't come eventually, because they will—but it's why we always reserve the right to wait and see, in case they're in no hurry to reveal themselves.

Back when I was first learning how to deal with my vampires, I was driving myself crazy over a decision about whether to keep a certain vampire in my life or not. At the time I had no experience with revoking my invitations, but I was, little by little, beginning to believe there were *some* vampires in my life that I might have the ability to do something about.

Being new to all this, I just assumed that as soon as someone perceived a vampire in their life, they were required to make a decision about whether or not to slay it. I further assumed that one should always want to slay one's vampires, since vampires were so obviously "bad," and we shouldn't want them around. I guess I thought it was a sort of a "see and slay" deal: like if I *saw* a vampire, I *had* to slay it—or that I should, at the very least, want to.

So when the day came when I recognized a vampire in my life, I thought I was supposed to know what I wanted to do about it right away. The only problem was, I didn't know. I couldn't decide. Even though I was pretty sure I had a vampire feeding on me, I still couldn't make up my mind about whether I wanted to revoke my invitation to it or not: I kept going back and forth on it.

Fortunately for me, I had another extraordinary Watcher at the time, named Catherine, who gave me this perfectly priceless piece of watcherly advice. She said:

"You don't have to make a decision today,"

and then repeated it as often as I needed to hear it.

So I took her word for it. I believed her, and instead of using the whip on myself for not being able to make my decision on a dime, I tried to relax and pay attention to what was happening in my everyday life. Like I'd pay attention to the shower I was taking or the clothes I was putting on, or I'd pay attention to the work I was doing or the cigarette I was smoking. And when I was brushing my teeth I would try to pay attention to brushing my teeth—things like that. And then one day, when I was very definitely *not* expecting it, I knew what I wanted to do about my vampire. One minute I didn't know, and then the next minute I knew for sure, and I was raking the leaves or something when it happened.

So the moral here, in case you missed it, is that none of us can be expected to make a decision before we're ready, and it's just plain silly to think that we should. If we've asked ourselves what we want to do and haven't gotten an answer, then *we're not ready*. In fact, "we're not ready" *is* the answer. And it makes way more sense to just go on with our lives, do our best, and trust that we will know what to do when we *are* ready.

The "wait and see" option grants a compassionate reprieve to the part of us that is freaking out about having to make up our minds right this second. It gives official and sympathetic notice to us that it is not only unrealistic but also painful to try and force ourselves to do a thing before we're ready to, no matter how much information we have and no matter how much we think we ought to be ready.

If we're not ready to make a decision today, then we're just not. It's okay. We don't have to take out the whip and beat ourselves because of it. Self-mutilation does not help us become better slayers; all it does is hurt. And what's practical about that?

Nothing, that's what. So let's try to relax and take it easy, shall we? And trust our inner timing, just for today.

3. Revoking Our Invitations

When we choose to revoke an invitation, it means we've decided to withdraw our permission for a particular vampire to enter. It means that we're putting that vampire on the other side of a closed door—outside of our lives—and that they can no longer come and go as they please. It means, in short, that their days of dropping in for a quick bite are over.

It doesn't mean that we destroy them, and the truth is that we can't actually stop them from knocking again—at least not ultimately, we can't—but we do make our thresholds clear to our vampires, and we do make it clear to them that we want them on the other side of those thresholds. Revoking an invitation is not like making a pact to keep them out forever—and in fact, making a "forever pact" is a lot more like slaying a vampire than revoking an invitation to one. But we'll be coming to that in a minute.

For some of us, deciding to revoke our invitation was just a matter of learning the vampire rules: Some of us have known for a long time that we had a vampire in our homes, but we didn't know it was our invitation that brought them in. Some of us knew we didn't want to live with our vampires any more, but we didn't know that we could revoke our invitations to them if we wanted them out.

Now, however, some of us know better. And if we want to be sure that we're ready to revoke our invitations, we can ask ourselves these questions first:

- Am I sure I'm done with my vampire, at least for now?
- Am I sure I understand my motives and what I stand to lose by revoking my invitation?
- Have I searched my heart and know that this is a risk I want to take?

If you are sure of all these things, you can move on to the next chapter to learn how. You're ready, and it's waiting.

4. Slaying the Vampire

There are, without a doubt, some vampires that require stronger eviction measures than our revocations alone. Whereas revoking an invitation is an appropriate solution to a vampire (or problematic relationship with someone) whose behavior toward us is, in part, a result of the way we've taught them (or invited them) to treat us, slaying a vampire requires a lifetime commitment to keeping them out of our lives and usually involves changing our own lives in ways to ensure the vampire does not return. It's a bigger deal, yes? Because that's not usually the kind of commitment we make when a neighbor is bothersome: most of the time a vampire like that can be dispatched with a well-thought-out, well-timed revocation—although even these, if persistent enough, will need reinforcement. But when the vampire is something like an addiction or has proven to be a life-threatening relationship (perhaps a domestic abuse situation), then it's time to consider immediate slaying. The vampires we slay are the ones we have *serious and permanent* bad reactions to—the kind of vampires we want to commit to keeping out of our lives for good.

If you think you're hosting a vampire that might require slaying, you can ask yourself these questions:

- Is this a vampire that comes first in my life, ahead of everyone I truly love? Is it an addiction (or *like* an addiction) that must be fed before anything else, even though I wish my loved ones came first?
- Have I ever risked my life to keep this vampire fed? If this is a violent or controlling person who's the vampire, have I ever been in physical danger or hospitalized because of them? If it's an addiction, have I ever been in an accident or hospitalized because of it? Have I risked my safety or the safety of others to make sure I got my addiction needs met?
- Are my loved ones concerned about my relationship with this vampire? Do I try to hide the truth about this vampire

from my loved ones and myself? Do I make excuses for it? Do I lie to cover up the damage its appetites cause?

- Am I scared to death to revoke my invitation, or does it seem impossible to either get away from or live without this vampire?
- Is this a vampire that seems like no big deal, but because I've attempted to revoke my invitation to them so many times now without effect, is starting to *become* a big deal?

If your answer to any of these questions was yes, slaying your vampire is an option for you to seriously consider. You may want to proceed to Chapter 10 on slaying the vampire. It could be the solution for you.

For now, though, when it comes to the options we have for disposing of our vampires, the list is this:

- We can *forgive* them.
- We can *wait and see* about them.
- We can *revoke our invitations* to them.
- Or we can *slay* them.

The choice is ours and, as usual, all we need to do is ask. The answer will come if we want it to—which reminds me of something Julie once said to me about questions and answers. She said, "All you have to do is ask the question. And if you find that you can't even bring yourself to ask it, or that you somehow never 'get around to' asking it, then you still get your answer: the answer being, of course, that you're not ready to know and don't even want to."

And I'm sure I don't need to tell you this, but I'm going to just the same: Finding out that we're not yet ready for an answer *is a perfectly good answer*. If we've come that far we've shown more courage than we probably realize, because whether we know it or not, we've picked up that stick of wood and started to whittle away at it. We've shown, at the very least, a willingness to know ourselves, and that's strong stuff, even when it's all we've got.

In fact, once we've come that far, I'm not even sure there's any turning back—and that's *also* a good thing. I promise.

Invisibility

Dear Slayer,

Lately I've been feeling unappreciated. When I take clean laundry into my kids' room and find it three hours later on the floor, or when I drive them places and they get out without so much as a "thank you," I just want to cry. I've never been this sensitive, but I feel like I'm starting to look for these things, and when I find them, my heart feels like it's going to break. What is my problem?

Signed,
Suddenly Touchy

Dear S.T.,

We all know that a vampire can't see its own reflection, and most of us have tried so hard and so fruitlessly to get our vampires to "see themselves" as to be utterly convinced of the truth of it. But when we, as hosts, put off revoking our invitations, we sometimes find that when *we* look in the mirror, too, all that's left is a dim shadow of our former selves. Sadly, we too start to disappear.

Lately I've heard a lot of stories about how awful it feels to do things for loved ones that go without acknowledgement: the dishes, the laundry, the cooking, the shopping, the patient listening—and I believe the absence of their gratitude can make us start to feel invisible ourselves, almost as if we're not even there. This is a very strong symptom of "vampire hosting," and one you ought to take seriously. When you are ready to find yourself again, dear reader, you can. All you need is still right there inside you, and this book is designed to help you find it.

With gratitude,
PVS

....

9

Choosing to Evict

Specific Instructions for Revoking Our Invitations

When we're addressing our vampires and particularly when we're revoking our invitations to them, as we know, clarity is essential. And the good news in this chapter is that if we've taken the time to get clear with ourselves about who we are and what we want, our revocation has, by now, practically written itself.

Once we diagnosed the presence of a vampire in our lives and decided we wanted to do something about it, we began to search earnestly inside ourselves for some answers. Taking care that we would not be interrupted, we went to where we could be either alone or with our Watcher, and then asked ourselves what we really wanted. Did we want to keep this vampire in our lives a while longer, or were we through with them? We reflected on the obstacles that had been in the way of our freedom: we shed light on all our fears and doubts about ending our vampire relationship, and on all our insecurities and ideas about what it would be like to live without them, too. We wrote these things down so we could keep track of our thoughts, and when we were through, we weighed our desire to be free of our vampire against our desire to hold on to these obstacles, and made our decision.

Some of us chose to forgive our vampires and to live with them, and some of us chose to give ourselves more time to decide. Some of us knew—and perhaps even long ago—that we wanted to revoke our invitations and were raring to go. Boy, were we ever ready. And all we needed now were the instructions.

The Heart of Practical Vampire Slaying

When we stop to think about vampires, slayers, and all the mythology surrounding them, it's kind of interesting to notice how often the subject of "the heart" comes up.

In one case, we talk about the *heart of the host*, which is the heart that determines what we desire for our lives and the lengths we're willing to go in order to fulfill that desire. When we tired of our vampires and finally asked ourselves what we truly wanted to do about them, it was our heart that provided the answers.

Then there is the *heart of the revocation*, which gives voice to the heart of the host. The heart of the revocation contains the exact expression of our heart's desire, telling the vampire precisely what we want or don't want in our relationship with them from now on. The heart of the revocation almost always contains the very words we've stopped ourselves from speaking in the past, fearing they were too abrupt or perhaps (ironically enough) too heart*less*. When we tried to soften the words or to ease their sting by buffering the truth or dropping hints instead, our vampires never seemed to get the point—as indeed, there was no point left for them *to* get. All that equivocating had dulled the point of the stake we'd intended to use down to nothing, making our revocations unusable and, well… point-*less*. Finally, we saw that there was no other way: we saw that if we wanted them to hear and respect our revocations, we were going to have to sharpen our words and speak directly to them from—of all places—our hearts.

Lastly and perhaps most famously, there is the *heart of the vampire*. As we all know, when slayers stake their vampires, they must always aim for the heart. And just as our revocations must be true and executed *without passion*, so the slayer's aim must be accurate and their attitude composed. If the stake should fall just a smidge to the left or a peep to the right, or if the slayer is so impassioned by their work that they become vulnerable to the vampire's thrall, then all will be lost and as legend has it, the vampire will rise again.

And some of us have had more than enough experience with that old "rising again" routine. We're way more familiar than we care to be with how it feels to drop our hints, miss our aim, and have our vampires come calling to feed again and again. We are in fact so sick of the whole cycle that we're ready to pick up our stakes, to pay attention, do the job right, and to do it for good this time.

So let's talk about that. Let's talk about how to revoke our invitations the right, permanent way.

Composing Revocations that Work

Effective revocations contain two elements that are indispensable. These are:

1. The heart of the revocation
2. An acknowledgement of our invitation

More often than not, but not always, they also contain a third element. This is:

3. The amends we may or may not want to make to our vampire

Sometimes they even contain a fourth element, but I'm going to keep quiet about that one until after we've covered the first three. It's personal.

1. The Heart of the Revocation

One of the nicest things about taking the time to check in with ourselves on the subject of who we are and what we really want is that, now that we're clear about all these things, it's just so much easier for us to express them to other people. Practically speaking, it's really rather nice to know what we mean to say before we open our mouths to say it, and really so much easier to explain what we want when we know what that is. This is especially true when we're revoking an invitation to a vampire.

The most common mistake I see among those of us who are attempting to revoke our invitations is that we always seem to be trying to say what we want to say without actually having to say it. Unrealistically enough, we want our vampires out the door, but we don't want to have to show them to it ourselves. So that's the first thing we need to get over if we're ever going to issue a revocation that works: wanting to have it both ways.

Nowhere in the world that I know of do people have much success in both doing a thing and not doing it at the same time. As far as I know, it's not possible to close a door and open it at the same time, nor is it possible to revoke an invitation and not revoke it at the same time. It doesn't work, and for as many times as we've probably tried that, you'd think by now we'd know.

You remember how I kept trying to do that with my old boyfriend? And remember how he could never hear me when I did? I blamed *him* for that—for not being able to hear me at the time—but the truth was that I wasn't being clear with him about wanting to end the relationship. As my Watcher pointed out to me, I'd been telling him that I *couldn't* be with him rather than telling him that I didn't *want* to be with him, and that made me guilty not only of trying to say a thing without saying it, but also of not making a clear statement of my will.

This is why you'll hear me keep harping on the importance of engaging our will in the revocation process. Any time we try to disengage our will from a revocation, our revocation will lose all its power—poof—just like that. No will = no power, and that's all there is to it.

I sympathize, of course, with what we're trying to do when we pull the heart out of our revocations: when we say we *can't* instead of saying we *won't*; when we say we wish we could instead of saying we don't want to, when we say yes instead of saying no—I mean, obviously we're trying to soften the blow and go easy on our vampires. But the result is that we corrupt the meaning of what we're trying to tell them so completely, they can't even begin to understand our message—a message they don't want to understand in the first place, remember. So there's no point in our being deliberately vague. It's positively ridiculous.

To begin with, if we think that the words "can't" and "won't" mean the same thing and are somehow interchangeable, then, as the saying goes, we've got another think coming.

Consider the following examples:

- *I can't swim.*
- *I don't want to swim.*

- *I can't go to the game.*
- *I don't want to go to the game.*

- *I can't have a relationship with you.*
- *I don't want to have a relationship with you.*

See what I mean?

Before I could revoke my invitation to my boyfriend, I had to take responsibility for my own will, which of course meant that I had to tell him what was truly in my heart. I had to tell him what I wanted, and so naturally, when I told him, "I can't have a relationship with you," he was never going to hear it. Only when I engaged my will and said, "I don't want to have a relationship with you," was I able to free myself. And him, by the way. Him, too.

Let's say, for instance, that we've identified our vampire as a neighbor who is forever popping over unannounced and who has failed take even one of the thousands of hints we've been dropping for her to knock it off. We've decided to revoke our invitation to this babe: we know what's in our hearts and that's just exactly what we're going to tell her, too. Thus, in our revocation to her, we would say:

"I don't want you coming over unannounced any more."

Yeah, I know ... and in fact, I can almost see you shaking your head from here, because it does look a little harsh when you see it all alone up there like that by itself. It can be hard to imagine saying anything like that. But this element, these words that identify exactly what we want or don't want from our vampires is only the *heart of the revocation*, and let me remind you: there's more to a revocation than just the heart of it.

So for clarity's sake, let's draw a table. We'll call it a "Revocation Table" and we'll keep adding new elements to it as we go along.

In this first table we'll be looking at the heart of the revocation and a few situations where it might be applied. While I realize that this part may seem obvious to some of you, you'd be amazed if you knew how many people I've talked to who practically have to take their tongues out of their mouths and physically twist them into position just to get the right words out—that's how hard it is for them to speak their own will. Plus: these things take practice, so in this first Table, just try and remember that. We want this way of talking to become as natural to us as tying our shoes.

REVOCATION TABLE 1.0
The Heart of the Revocation

WHEN REVOKING AN INVITATION TO	INSTEAD OF SAYING	FROM NOW ON, WE'LL SAY
Girlfriend/boyfriend we want to break up with	"I can't have a relationship with you any more."	"I don't want to have a relationship with you any more."
Neighbor who borrows our stuff all the time... and I do mean *all* of the time	"Do you still have my frying pan/green sweater/copy of *The Great Gatsby*? It was a special gift to me and I really need to have it back if you don't mind."	"Would you please return my frying pan/green sweater/ *The Great Gatsby*?"
Telemarketer or some other stranger calling for our money at dinnertime	"I can't afford it." "I'm in the middle of dinner." "I'm not interested." "I don't need that."	"Would you please take my name off your calling list?
Friend who calls us on the phone A LOT and then wants to talk for*ever*	"I can't talk right now." "I have to make dinner." "I have to put the kids to bed." "I'm sick."	"I don't want to spend this much time on the phone with you."

(Continued on next page)

REVOCATION TABLE 1.0 (*continued*)

WHEN REVOKING AN INVITATION TO	INSTEAD OF SAYING	FROM NOW ON, WE'LL SAY
Friend or person who regularly insults or "teases" us and when we get mad about it accuses us of being "too sensitive" or insists they were "just kidding"	"Screw you," OR "(*Something worse*) you" OR responding by: • Laughing along with them • Saying nothing • Pouting • Insulting them right back • Gossiping about them	"I don't want you to talk that way about me."

The statements in the last column reflect and state the will of the host and are, as you know, the heart of each revocation. Instead of dropping hints or trying to cover the truth about our will, we make certain that everybody (including us) understands that we're not saying this "just because we're mad," and that we're not apologizing for saying it, either. We're not suggesting in any way that this is something we have to do or can't afford, not something we would-do-if-we-could-do, and it's also not something that we *might* be able to do later. It's none of those things. Nothing is out of our control and nothing is happening against our will. What we are telling them is what we want, and that's it. Even if we do have to wrestle with our tongues just a little bit to get it out.

2. Acknowledgement of Our Invitation

If we've surveyed our inner landscape thoroughly, then we have, at least hopefully, discovered some important truths about who we really are and what it is that we've really been up to. Hopefully we've begun to see the responsibility we need to take in the relationship we've been having with this person. Hopefully we've started to see how we invited them in, and hopefully, too, we've begun to identify the ways in which we've left the door open to them ever since we invited them in. So this is the next part we include in our revocation, the part we'll be referring to, from now on, as "our part."

When we talk about our part in a relationship or situation, we are of course referring to the part that we've played and the things we've done in that relationship or situation. When it comes to our vampires and how we compose our revocations to them, this is where we acknowledge our invitations to them—or, to put it plainly: this is where we own up to the fact that they didn't get in without a little help from us.

Some of us might have trouble acknowledging that they've miscalculated, misjudged, or even erred in this respect. Understandably apprehensive about having to take responsibility for any mistakes they might make, they are in the careful habit of justifying their actions rather than acknowledging them. There are people in whom this habit is so deeply ingrained that they've even come to think of "justifying their actions" and "acknowledging their actions" as being the same thing.

These misguided boneheads can usually be heard making acknowledgements of responsibility that sound something like this:

> *"Yeah, I stole that guy's money, but he was such a creep that he really kind of owed it to me."*

As you can see: some of us have a little problem with making this distinction between reporting what they do and rationalizing what they do. But in their defense I have to say that it's really hard to tell the truth when you have no idea what the truth is. It's like being in another dimension. You can't see yourself, so you don't think anyone else can, either. Some people imagine that if they have a good enough reason for *doing wrong*, that it's somehow less likely to be viewed as *wrongdoing*.

As I say, it's like another dimension.

Effective revocations require clear thinking and precise language. For most of us that means we're going to have to learn the difference between reporting the facts and rationalizing the facts. Contrary to our habitually defensive impulses, the two are not the same and, in fact, do not even "go together." When we attempt to muffle our acknowledgements of responsibility by padding them with all the good reasons we had for erring in the first place, our responsibility gets lost. And not a slayer in the world can possibly hope to move forward without a willingness to take responsibility for what they do.

So let's go back now to our friend who said he stole money from a guy because the guy had it coming: let's just pretend that, rather than trying to justify himself, he'd been trying to acknowledge responsibility for his actions instead. If that had been the case, he probably would have said something a lot more like this:

"I stole ten bucks from that guy."

See the period at the end of that sentence? That's his ticket to freedom, right there. The secret to figuring out where to put the period (or stop talking) is simply to pay attention to the moment when we've *stopped talking about ourselves*. If, in the midst of taking responsibility for what we've done or failed to do, we hear ourselves talking about someone else and how much responsibility *they* need to take for our actions, then it's time to back up, delete the part about that other guy, and then start over. This is about our responsibility and only ours.

When it comes to acknowledging responsibility for our actions, we're the only subjects that count. This is true in life and also true when it comes to acknowledging the invitations we've extended to our vampires. It is obviously not enough for us to say, "I invited the vampire in because he tricked me," any more than it is enough to say, "I never would have behaved like such a jerk if not for the vampire"—*even if that's true.*

This is important. Because, really, you guys: how sick of passing the buck do we have to get before we finally, as a society, put our feet on the ground and start behaving like responsible adults instead of children trying to blame everybody else for their actions? Enough. If we want to be players, then we're going to have to get in the game—and that means *all* the time, not just when we're winning, right? So let's go back now to our popping-in neighbor and the revocation we're composing for her. Let's think about the part we've played in our relationship with her: about how we invited her in and how we might have led her to believe that she was still welcome long after we were so sick of her we were ready to start hiding in the shower whenever she called—which we would in fact have done, if only we'd thought we could get away with it. Let's consider our invitation to her and what we might need to say in order to acknowledge it.

We can begin by asking ourselves these questions (that's right; it's notebook time again! This is the stuff we want in black and white where we can see it):

- How did we invite the vampire in? What words or gestures did we use? What were we thinking when we invited them in to begin with? Were we genuinely interested in them, or were we just trying to live up to some perception we had of ourselves as being "the gracious neighbor" or something like that?
- Are we guilty of unintentionally misleading our vampire? How did our actions and words convey to the vampire that it was fine with us if they kept coming back any old time? What message were we sending when we starting

dropping hints that we wanted to see less of them instead of simply speaking to them from our hearts?

We search our memories for these answers and, as I say, there's a good chance we've already discovered many of them during the time we spent in quiet contemplation or discussion with our Watchers, so we may not have far to look. As I said earlier: if we have taken the suggested steps up to this point, our revocations really have almost written themselves. We've got the goods.

If, in considering these questions, we can honestly say that our part and responsibility really were limited to the (perhaps unrealistic) expectations we had when we invited her in and to how we later misled her—to how, by our behavior, we made it look like her dropping over just any old time was fine and dandy with us; if our self-examination shows us that it was primarily our acts of omission that got us into trouble, and if it was by failing to speak the truth that we hurt not only ourselves but the vampire, too, then our amended revocation might look something like this:

"When you moved in next door and I invited you into my home, I thought our visits would be planned, and that we would agree to them before you came over. Unfortunately, it hasn't been happening that way, and I want to say that I'm sorry; because I think I might have misled you by acting like these unplanned visits were okay with me. I'd like to be clear and honest with you about that now: They're really not okay with me and **I don't want you coming over unannounced any more."**

See that part where the words are in bold? Remember that? That's the good old heart of the revocation we were talking about earlier. Do you see how our honesty concerning the role we played in this misunderstanding has not only broadened the truth, but softened it, too? Isn't that lovely? Isn't that just the coolest?

Okay. It's table time again.

Revocation Table 1.1

Adding Our Acknowledgement

When Adding an Acknowledgment of Our Invitation to	Instead of saying	From Now On, Say
Girlfriend/boyfriend we want to break up with	**"I can't keep seeing you and talking to you like this any more, it's driving me crazy.** I can't have a relationship with you any more."	**"I'm sorry if my actions have been confusing to you, and I regret that by continuing to see and talk with you I've made my feelings unclear. I want to correct that now.** I don't want to have a relationship with you any more."
Neighbor who borrows our stuff all the time... and I do mean all the time	**"Gosh, I'm sorry, but I've really been missing my frying pan/green sweater/copy of** *The Great Gatsby*! **Do you think you're going to be done with them any time soon?** It was a special gift and I really have to have it back if you don't mind."	**"I'm sorry if by lending you my things that I gave you the impression it was okay for you to borrow things so often, and I'd like to clear that misunderstanding up now: I don't want to lend my things to you any more, and I'd prefer if in the future you wouldn't ask me.** And would you please return my frying pan/green sweater/*The Great Gatsby*?"

(Continued on next page)

Revocation Table 1.1 (*continued*)

When Adding an Acknowledgment of Our Invitation to	Instead of Saying	From Now On, Say
Telemarketer or someone else calling for our money at dinnertime	**"You're calling me right in the middle of dinner with my family! How would you like it if I called YOU at your home all the time? ___ you!** I can't afford it." "I'm in the middle of dinner." "I'm not interested." "I don't need that."	"Would you please take my name off your calling list?
Friend who calls us A LOT and then never wants to let us off the phone.	**"You're always calling me at the worst times! Can't you give me a break once in a while and quit bugging me so much?"** "I can't talk right now." "I have to make dinner." "I have to put the kids to bed." "I'm sick."	**"You know, I think that by spending so much time on the phone with you that I've been giving you the wrong message, and I'm sorry I've misled you. It probably seems to you like I want to spend this much time on the phone, but I'd like to clear up this misunderstanding right now:** I don't want to spend this much time on the phone with you."
Friend or person who regularly insults us and when we get mad about it accuses us of being "too sensitive" and insists they were "just kidding"	**"Screw you,"** OR "You're the biggest *bleep*hole on the planet." OR responding by: • Laughing along with them • Saying nothing • Pouting • Insulting them right back • Gossiping about them	**"I regret not telling you this sooner, because I think I've given you the wrong impression about I way I feel, and I want to put an end to that misunderstanding right now:** I don't want you to talk that way about me."

The addition of our acknowledgement is in bold in the last column, and it comes right before the heart of the revocation, as you can see. You'll notice that in each case, the only fault we're admitting is in misleading our vampires by our past words and actions ... *except for one*. Did you notice the exception?

The exception to the rule is the telemarketer. This is because when it comes to telemarketers and their kin, we're going to want to take control of the conversation (i.e. *"Would you please take my name off your calling list?"*) not only immediately but also permanently. Once we've established control, we're not going to want to risk losing it by allowing the subject to be changed or by changing it ourselves. When it comes to telemarketers, it's necessary to plant our feet firmly and not be moved.

Please understand: I'm not saying that if we personally feel we owe them an apology or if we have a part in our invitation or misleading them that we need to take responsibility for that we shouldn't go ahead and do so: by all means, we should. Each of us knows best what part of the responsibility we share: it's our house, our invitation, and our power we're talking about here, after all.

My recommendation, however—as a general rule—is to at all costs maintain control of the subject when talking to these guys, and the subject (if we're revoking our invitation to them) is *that we want to be taken off their lists*. We avoid letting them pull all their sidetracking tricks, and we try to stay in control. Or at least I do.

3. The Amends We May or May Not Want to Make to Our Vampire, and a Word or Two About Confession:

I heard a guy (okay, he was a priest, I'll admit it) say one time that we make amends for our mistakes so that we may bring the scales of God's justice back into balance. Call me a sap, but I can't think of a better reason, or a prettier one either, for making peace with my fellows and my world—vampires included.

It is simply not enough for us to know that we want to put an end to our relationship with our vampire and to then just go ahead and revoke our invitations to them; we have to clean up any mess we've made that's associated with that vampire, too. We have to find our part in this unwholesome relationship we've been having, and then we have to find our part of the mess or imbalance we've caused (if any) in the world because of it.

Twelve-step programs are kind of famous for this: they talk about the importance of members finding "their part" in the unhealthy or undesirable relationships they have, and about the importance of making amends for their participation in those relationships, too.

And it's true: when I lied to people about my drinking and using, when I tried to cover up where I was going and what I was doing, and most especially when the things I did and the lies I told resulted in what must have been agonizing worry for the people who loved me, it *was* due to my disease and my relationship with alcohol and drugs. No doubt about it. I never would have done those things without the disease driving me to do them. That's for sure.

But here's the thing: That still doesn't make me any less responsible for the mess I made, even if the disease was the driving force behind it. I'm still responsible for the imbalance I caused, and I see it that way, too—as an imbalance or disorder: a disturbance, like ... *in the Force*. That's such a good way to think about it: as a disturbance in the force or an imbalance in the scales of justice.

There were people I hurt and stole from, there were people I was mean or just plain rude to, and then there was the damage I did to their homes, their businesses, and most especially there was the damage I did to their hearts and to their ability to trust not only me, but other people and things, too. I mean, even strangers were affected: maybe they were people trying to play in the park with their kids and there I was, intoxicated and making a scene, or maybe there were people whose lives and the lives of whose children I threatened every time I was drinking and then got behind the wheel of a car. I don't even know how many people I harmed, really, but I do know I affected their lives. And it's like that priest said: *there is a balance*—in life, in God's justice, in the Force, or whatever you want to call it—and the things I did when I was drinking and using threw that balance off. In terms of justice, it just doesn't matter one bit whether I did them because of a disease or not.

Can you just imagine how absurd it would be for me to say, "I did those things because of the disease so I guess the rest of you are just going to have to suck it up," and then expect that to settle the score or to make things right? How would that put back into order the things I'd disturbed or clean up the mess? How would that restore any balance to the scales of justice? How would that calm a disturbance in the Force? I mean, after the earthquake, it's time to sweep the floor and straighten the pictures, right? We don't just say, "Well, it wasn't *my* fault," and then leave the mess there.

Once we've seen our part in how we invited our vampires in and acknowledged as much in our revocations, there are just a few more questions we need to answer so we can complete our work with confidence and integrity (still whittling that stake, you betcha). They are:

1. How, if at all, did we harm our vampire?
2. Was there any wrong we committed against them that we justified by telling ourselves they deserved it or had it coming for all the trouble they've caused us?
3. Did we lie to them, gossip about them, steal from them, or harm them in some other way that we've forgotten? And if we did, how specifically were they hurt and how specifically will we make reparations to them?

We consider these since this is another grave danger we need to be aware of when we host a vampire: that our resentment about the vampire will cause us to behave badly and then rationalize that bad behavior, too. Remember: to say that our vampires had it coming or that we never would have done these things if not for the vampire *will not suffice*. That kind of thinking does nothing to restore order and balance in our lives or the lives of anyone else, and what's more, it reinforces those old beliefs we once had that we were strictly victims and that our vampires had all the power. Which was nonsense, of course.

There have been many times in my life where, by just seeing and adding the truth about my part to a revocation, the whole encounter has become so much less scary and awkward for me. It seems that there are times when, instead of simply telling our vampires the truth about our wanting them out, it is better for everyone if we tell them the whole truth—which includes the part, if any, that we played in how our relationship with them failed.

Let's say that in our self-examination, we found instances where we lied to, stole from, gossiped about, or cheated this person. What if, in the case of that neighbor, for instance, we told ourselves that because she was so obnoxious, it was okay for us to ask her for money and not pay it back, or to borrow her things and never return them? What if we took things from her and "forgot about them" or told ourselves it was okay since she "really sort of owed them to us anyway," or because we just plain old had no respect for her?

Well, from my point of view, this would be a situation where we would 'fess up and pay the money back or return the items that we (as Kurt Vonnegut once so adorably put it) "borrowed for all eternity." This would be a case where I'd want to balance the scales by returning the money (with interest, if necessary), or the clothing (and if damaged or worn out by use, replacing or paying for it). In this instance, there can be no harm in telling our vampire the whole truth about our part and doing our best to set things right. No one will be hurt or even potentially hurt by settling an account such as this.

Our revocation, in that situation, might look something like this (formatted for clarity; please and for heaven's sakes, do not include numbers or odd-sounding pauses indicating the use of numbers in your speech):

1. "There are a couple of things I feel have been out of order in our relationship and some mistakes I've made that I'd like to correct now, if I can."
2. "I want to tell you that: *over the past few months/years/or that one time*"
   (When)
3. "I took *this money/these items*"
   (What)
4. "And now I'd like to *pay you back/return the item*"
   (Make these reparations)
5. "This was wrong of me to do, and I apologize sincerely for it."

6. "Another matter I'd like to discuss is our relationship: when I first invited you over I imagined we'd see each other occasionally and by prior agreement, but I believe you understood it differently—imagining that it was fine to drop over anytime without arranging to first—and I want you to know that I do not want to continue this way. I apologize for misleading you by pretending that it was all right with me for you drop over without calling first—and now I want to be very clear with you about it."
7. "It's really not okay with me, and the truth is that I don't want you coming over unannounced from now on."

Now, please remember this model is designed only to demonstrate the elements that make up a thorough revocation, and that each of us finds our own best words to use. The idea here is to be clear, first about our part: for us to admit the specific harm we've done (1, 2, 3), and then to pay back the money or return the items on the spot (4), and apologize (5).

Having covered that part of our amends, we then continue by admitting any harm we've done in misleading them (6), and explain exactly what we want (or usually *don't* want) from them in the future: this is again where our old friend *the heart of the revocation* (7) comes in.

That's one example: one where our amends are primarily of a material nature. But as we know, there are other harms we do to people, and some of those we may not want to be as candid about. In fact, there are harms that, in our attempt to make amends for them, can cause even more harm—which is not what we're setting out to do here.

When We Need to Acknowledge Our Wrongs, but NOT to Our Vampires

What if, in all our frustration with our vampire over these months or years, we've complained to other people about our vampire and their reputation has been hurt by our words? Is our honesty so imperative that we must go to our vampire and tell them the exact content of the gossip and all the details of who was there and what was said? What if we gossiped about them and told ourselves at the time that it was okay since, because of their own bad behavior, they had it coming? How would *that* amends fit into our revocation? Would it fit at all, or do we just say, "Screw 'em, they're vampires," and leave it at that? Hmm?

As always and in the end, it's going to be our own personal call, however: I *do* think a very good rule of thumb to follow is this: *We admit to our vampire only as much as will serve a good purpose.* Once our confession starts to risk hurting someone, even our vampire, then it's time to *stop talking.* We certainly don't wish to cause more harm by telling them something that would only hurt them more. Not only is spilling our guts about everything ineffective in terms of any kind of universal balance we're trying to recover, but it also has the potential for putting into motion a never-ending cycle of interaction with this person and a bunch of big, fat complications for us and other people, besides.

Because what if we did tell them that we gossiped about them? Then the chances are pretty good they're going to want to know exactly what was said and to whom—and once we reveal that information, then they're probably going to go rushing off to those people to interrogate and bother them—which certainly falls into the category of causing harm to others from where I sit. When our confession to the vampire has the potential to cause more trouble than it may cure, the smart thing to do is to say nothing, at least to them.

Besides: *Never* do we want to the kind of person who says, "I just tell the truth and if people can't handle it, that's their problem." Phooey. Yuck. *Nev-er*. People who think and talk that way don't have the slightest idea what's really happening, and are disconnected in a way that's awful to contemplate.

There are some amends that are better left unspoken, or at least to the people and vampires we've offended, however, and here it comes: although there are plenty of situations where we shouldn't admit all to our vampires, we should probably admit all to *somebody*: somebody who will not be affected or hurt in any way by the content of what we're confessing.

Confession

This principle of confession comes up in Stephen King's *'Salem's Lot*: When the band of slayers are preparing to slay the master vampire, there's a priest among them named Father Callahan who insists that each slayer make a confession of their sins before they go—and I always used to wonder about that. Why would a slayer want to make a confession before facing their vampires?

Then I remembered about our vampires' 20/20 night vision and how, if we haven't made a confession and brought our private failings into the light, then all those vulnerabilities, weaknesses, limitations, and mistakes we've left out are just sitting there for our vampires to see and take advantage of.

The trouble with confession is that if we don't do it, then we're not only vulnerable to the vampire we're dealing with today, but we're also vulnerable to every other hungry predator from now until doomsday. As long as we leave our blind spots and susceptibilities out there in the dark, then any opportunistic n'er-do-well can see them and use them against us any time they want to.

For many of us, the choice of confessor will be our Watcher or closest friend—someone who has experience and has done a little vampire slaying of his or her own. It will be someone who understands our purpose and won't be trying to mess with our agenda. For some it might be our psychologist, and for others a priest or member of the clergy who knows what we're doing and will listen with closed mouths. It will be our choice, as always—but we'll do well to keep in mind that the candidate for the job should be neutral, and above all *will not be hurt or otherwise affected by the content of our confession.*

To put it another way, in the name of all that's sane, we do not make our confession to our parents, spouses, children, or anyone else who might be hurt. And I wish I could say that I've never heard of anyone making such an unbelievably stupid move as that before, but I can't. I knew a guy who one time who thought it would be a good idea to make his confession to his mother. So I'm just saying: please think before acting—in this case especially.

It is crucial in ways we may not even understand that we say out loud what we've learned about ourselves and all we've kept hidden, and to say it in front of another person especially. When we've committed an offense against our vampire like theft or character assassination or when it comes to things we're perhaps very ashamed of and don't wish to repeat, a witness—or confessor—can be an almost magical thing to have.

Our witness reaffirms our intention to change, and to hear our story told out loud to another person has healing properties so powerful and exponential that they've been well known and practiced in psychology, religion, and just plain old healthy relationships since just about forever. Confession is strong medicine, which may be why so many of us hesitate to take it. But if we are serious about our slaying, we'll do it, and in time we may even come to desire it, too.

One more thought about this: while we're there with our Watcher or other chosen confessor it might also be a good idea to get their input on the question of whether or not we have any more amends to make.

In the example of gossiping, for instance, although we might decide it's best not to tell the offended party of our specific offense, it could be a very good thing to go to the people we gossiped to, and to tell them we were wrong to speak that way about anyone, even if they are a vampire to us.

But see, then again, it might not—which is exactly why it's such a good idea to bounce this sort of question off a Watcher, confessor, or trusted friend—someone whose had experience with and knows the principles of practical vampire slaying and of making amends. I think when it comes to our amends it can be difficult to see the whole picture alone. We usually have some prejudice we're not even aware of and it muddies our perception of the right course to take. Then, too, there is the danger of our being too hard on ourselves, which is also not our purpose. Our purpose is to make peace with the God of our understanding, with ourselves, and with our brothers and sisters (which includes our vampires). An honest talk with another slayer or Watcher who has experience and perspective can help us to take it easy on ourselves and choose the best course.

The same rules apply to sexual indiscretions and any other situations where third parties are concerned, especially third parties who could easily be harmed by the overuse of our mouths or our misguided conviction that "we need to make a clean breast of things."

Once again: we try to think these things through carefully so that when we're done, it is peace we've made, and not more trouble.

4. That Fourth Element I Said Was Optional

The experiences I've had with invitation revoking and vampire slaying have affected my life quite a bit more than I anticipated. All of the self-examination, truth seeking, and truth telling involved in the process has led to a change in outlook that I really wasn't bargaining for when I started out. All I thought I wanted when I began was to find a way that worked to get rid of the relationships in my life that were so troublesome to me, but like so many other things in life, the road to my destination was not as straight as I'd anticipated. The road, in fact, was almost nothing like what I'd imagined at all.

One of the surprises I had after I'd revoked my invitation to my boyfriend and made amends for my part in the failure of our relationship, was that I discovered, a few months later, that I felt a strong desire *to thank him*. I wanted to thank him not only for all of the good times we'd had, but also for all the stuff I'd learned in the times we'd shared that hadn't been so good. I just wanted to thank him for our relationship, and for all that had encompassed.

Talk about your unexpected endings: I felt gratitude. Gratitude is the fourth possible element in our revocation, and I'm sure you can see now why I said it was a personal matter.

If we have found, in the study of our own heart and maybe even as a result of becoming free of this unhealthy relationship we've been having, feelings of gratitude for that person, then I think it's worth noting, and I think that it could even be worth sharing with them. I can tell you that in my case it has usually been after some time has passed since my revocation that I begin to feel this gratitude—and I should no doubt tell you, too, that there are times when it's perfectly appropriate to voice that gratitude, and times when it's perfectly inappropriate, too. In the case of my ex-boyfriend, for instance, it was perfectly safe and, I felt, appropriate to express. Much time had passed since our breakup, we had both started brand new and wonderful lives for ourselves, and I felt there could be no harm in my expressing my gratitude for all the experiences we'd shared.

But in the case of old Ted, the guy who kept showing up just before dinner, it was never appropriate to express my gratitude (even though I did and do feel it—and sadness, too), because it would have opened the door to him again. He was one vampire I never wanted crossing my threshold again, and I had enough evidence in my relationship with him to know that he would always be a vampire to me no matter what. To speak with him at all would have been a mistake, and so I never did again.

We'll be talking some more about gratitude and the role it plays in vampire slaying in our last two chapters, and leave the discussion right here. If we should come to a time in our slaying journey where we feel gratitude and want to express it, we'll know it; but for now, I just want to say that it can happen. When we want our lives to change and have a willingness to do a little work, it is my experience that almost anything can happen.

But that's life for you, especially when we're trying new things: it's always a good idea, just in case, and as the saying goes, to hang on to our hats.

Ask the Slayer

SHAPESHIFTING

Dear Slayer,

How do I get rid of a vampire in my life who is catty to me when we are alone, and then all cutesy and nice when my husband is around so he really likes her?

And here's what worries me: Did I make her into a vampire?

Grossed Out in New York

Dear Grossed Out,

Talk about efficiency in vampires! It sounds like this one has found a way to feed on your husband's attention and on your frustration at the same time. She's doing something we slayers call *shapeshifting*. Remember how Dracula could turn into a bat or a wolf or smoke? That's what she's doing, too: using that famously handy vampire power to shift shape so she can feed as much as possible.

It can be tricky getting rid of her since you might revoke your invitation to her in one shape, and then have her show up on your doorstep again in another shape, asking for another invitation—and if she catches you when you're not paying attention, you might give her that invitation she's seeking. You see the problem.

The solution is to turn the light not on her but on you. Bring your motive for retaining this "friendship" into the light where you can see it, and ask yourself if the reason you're keeping her around is really worth it. As for your "making her into a vampire," the answer is no. You don't have the power to do that. Only another vampire has the power to do that, and if you still have the ability to turn the light on yourself and look in the mirror, you're not one of those.

PVS

....

10

Choosing to Slay

The Way to a Permanent Solution

NO ONE SLAYS A VAMPIRE UNLESS THEY have to. It's a serious, back-against-the-wall, last resort kind of business, and one we turn to only after every other option, including our revocations, has failed. People who slay their vampires have come to the end of the line: they are out of ideas, strategies, and patience—but more than anything else, they are out of the willingness they once had to be hurt by their vampires. The scales have finally tipped, and whatever benefit they might have received by staying in relationship with the person or thing that has robbed them of so much has finally been outweighed. The blood-loss stops now, and for good.

When we make the decision to slay a vampire, there is no ceremony or fanfare, there is no pretty costume to wear or fancy stake for us to show off, and almost none of us feel happy about it. When the neighbor we've asked to stop dropping over refuses to comply, when the drinking or drug abuse we made a decision to control will not be governed, when the abusive spouse we've been living with has made it undeniably clear that they will never stop, or when our own obsessive thoughts or impulses are eating us alive and there is nothing we can do to restrain them, then—if we have clearly revoked our invitations and still they keep coming back—they have, in effect, thrown down the gauntlet. They've declared war, and it's time for us to bite back.

Knowing that the time to fight has come never feels that great, especially since it almost always coincides with our end-of-the-line exhaustion. And while on the one hand that probably sounds depressing and not nearly as glamorous or exciting as we might have hoped the prospect of slaying would feel, on the other, only monsters or fools rush into war before it's absolutely necessary, and only children or terribly sick people imagine that it might be fun.

Even so, the people I've witnessed slay their vampires are heroes in the truest sense: they see clearly and do what is necessary, even in the face of all their worst fears. Even when it means they must take their next step into what appears to be thin air, they go on—and guess what? The ground materializes beneath their feet, every time.

The truest and most beautiful words I've ever heard used to describe the way it feels to go to war with a life-threatening vampire came from a recovering alcoholic I heard about who once said, "I'm an alcoholic, and neither proud nor ashamed."

This is precisely the attitude we need to acquire, not only about our vampires, but also about ourselves. We need to see both for what they really are, no more, no less, and without pride or shame clouding our vision. Although we may feel tired or beaten even before we start, if we hold this attitude we'll discover an inner strength we never even guessed was there, a source of personal power that will keep us on the path we've chosen—which, for us, is the one to freedom.

The Vampires We Slay

There are two types of vampires that qualify for slaying: the first are those that threaten to destroy our **peace of mind** if we continue to stay in relationship with them, and the second are those that threaten to destroy our **lives** if we continue to stay in relationship with them.

Those Who Threaten Our Peace of Mind

In this first group we find people like a neighbor who, in spite of our revocations, still won't stop asking if she can leave her kids with us, drop over unannounced, or borrow things all the time. They are people like the coworker we've asked to stop talking while we're trying to concentrate at work, the telemarketer we've asked to stop phoning us entirely, and that guy or gal whose flirtation with us has crossed the line from being sweet and fun to being pushy and a little disgusting.

When we issue clear and well-timed revocations to these people or their specific behaviors and are rebuffed, it tells us we're dealing with a person who doesn't understand free will, and simply cannot comprehend it when we explain that we intend to exercise ours, and we want to either change or end our relationships with them. By their refusal, they are telling us they intend to fight—not for what is theirs, but for what is ours—and that they seriously mean to dispute our right to run our own lives. It would be funny, really, if it weren't such a pain—and although we can be pretty sure that their continued talking, borrowing, calling, and flirting won't kill us, we can be pretty sure, too, that it's not about to stop. Not without a little more help from us, it's not.

Those Who Threaten Our Lives

The consequences of allowing this second group to continue as they have are of course much more severe, and if nothing changes will eventually kill us. These include the physically and emotionally abusive partners, spouses, relatives, or friends who hurt us and refuse to stop. They are the addictions to alcohol, drugs, shopping, over- and under-eating, gambling, or anything else that dominates us and we cannot control. They are the compulsive thoughts or beliefs we have that torture us, and that we cannot restrain no matter how hard we try.

The damage they do in our lives is exponential and apparent to almost anyone who sees us. Even a five-year-old can see a black eye and detect the fear that lives behind it, and even a total stranger can smell alcohol and guess what's going on when we're unable to stand up straight or to speak without slurring our words. If we think we're keeping a secret, once again, we've got another think coming.

This deadly breed of vampire brings with it legal, financial, emotional, and physical problems that affect not only us, but also our families and loved ones—which sadly and for many of us, include our children. Through what has felt like nearly endless trial and error, we've discovered that we do not possess the power to influence these people or things, nor do we have the strength to close the door on them.

As believers in the insatiability of the vampire's appetite, we know they will never stop until there is nothing left, and as recipients of the gift of free will, we also know that the decision to evict them permanently from our lives belongs to us. It is in our hands, a part of the free will we've been granted with the deepest love there is and by the ultimate Watcher—the very same One who will restore us to freedom from our vampires, if we're willing to take that chance.

The Essentials

Vampire slaying is of course more involved than revoking an invitation, and that may be one reason so many people choose to continue living with theirs: they assume the process of slaying a vampire takes some work—and they're right about that. It does.

There are four elements to successful vampire slaying. They are:

1. An honest willingness to ask for and receive help
2. A new and specific plan for living without the vampire
3. Commitment
4. Power

Let's take a closer look at these, one at a time.

Willingness and Honesty

For many of us, having a problem like domestic abuse or addiction can be something we're ashamed of. This is a result of misunderstanding, of course: there is absolutely no shame at all in the love we have for *anyone*—even our abusers. There is no shame in the hope we have that they might change, and none in the fact that we put up with their abuse as long as we did. Each of us does what we feel we have to until we're finished with it, and any person who says otherwise or dares to criticize our timing has never looked closely in a mirror and studied their own reflection.

As far as our addictions go, too, there is no shame in contracting a disease, and no matter what the nature of our addiction is, it's always a disease. There is no shame in having a disease that has to run its course, and no shame in having to do what we do until we're done with it, either. Again, anyone who says otherwise and feels in a position to judge us is either blind or asking for trouble—probably both.

Still, for so many of us that shame exists, and exists so powerfully that it stops us from letting other people know the truth about our illness and asking for help. Remember what that guy said about "being neither ashamed nor proud?" That shame we feel is part of what he was talking about—the part we need to let go of.

Willingness to ask for help, for most of us, is born of necessity. When our ideas and energy have expired and we've got nothing left, that's when we open first our minds, and then our address books and the yellow pages: we call a friend, a doctor, the clergy, a loved one, or we find a Watcher: someone who has experience with our problem, knows a solution, and will be able to help and support us. When we're just starting out, we might begin with our best friend or person we trust most, and ask them to assist us in finding the help or specialist we need. The most important thing at this point is our confidence in this person: that we find someone we know has our back and will not try to take over or run the show; someone we're sure won't rush out to tell other people or in any way dramatize our situation, but who will instead simply assist us in finding our own path.

Honesty is crucial at this point, so when we tell our story to whomever will help us, we do our best to be honest and thorough. We tell the doctor, counselor, group, organization, or specialist we've found the *whole truth* about what's happening to us, even if it is uncomfortable. Remember: we're coming into the light and we want to be as specific as we can, giving our trusted helpers the clearest picture possible so the help they lead us to will be the best fit they can find.

The next part is a little trickier, though, because after we've described our situation and asked for help, we then have to be *willing to receive* the help we've asked for—and there are times when our pride gets in the way of that. Sometimes we'll hear a part of us whispering that we still know better than they do, and we revise their advice to suit ourselves.

We can do that if we want, but let's not con ourselves while we're doing it: if we revise the plan, we won't be receiving the help we've asked for—it will have been transformed, and that's why I say this part can be so tricky. Heaven knows it's hard to give the reins over to another person, especially when we're trying to get out from under the control of a vampire. Having recently suffered the damage that comes with having a vampire run our lives, it's not so easy to just jump in and trust someone else to do it. This is why we choose carefully, and with the help of someone who cares for us: so we can trust and receive the help that's given. If we don't, I'm afraid all we'll have done is asked for help and rejected it, and we'll end up feeding the same old vampire all over again.

The nice thing here is that if we really do take their advice, then we've probably adopted our first real Watcher—the one who knows all about this new path we're on and will walk it with us, and that's a good thing, because then it's official: not only will we be in the light, but also and from now on, we won't be alone.

If you are so unfamiliar with how it feels to be willing and wondering if you're really receiving the help you've asked for (have I been there? Yes, I have), there are some clues in your behavior you can watch for:

- When you find yourself no longer pondering, considering, or promising to take the advice you've asked for.

- When, instead of doing all that thinking and making a bunch of promises about what you'll be willing to do tomorrow, you find yourself actually *doing those things today*, that's a very good sign. Depending on your situation, it could be a million different things: but whether it's keeping in touch with others like yourself who are looking for help, or going to meetings or appointments designed to help you, taking walks or meeting friends for coffee—whatever it is, and much to your surprise you find yourself doing it, it's probably pretty safe to say you're both willing to receive and receiving the help you've asked for.
- When what you're doing feels so new it reminds you of learning how to walk or ride a bike for the first time, then you'll know for sure. When you feel like that, it's the strongest proof you'll ever get: you'll feel it in your heart, and you might be so excited that you can hardly stand it. But you can. It's just that sometimes feeling great can take a little getting used to, that's all.

A New Plan

When we're seeking a new and specific plan for living without our old unhealthy relationships, we're acknowledging that this person or problem has actually become a way of life to us, and even when the problem is one as seemingly minor as a neighbor whose habits have been driving us a little nuts, we still need a plan for how to keep her off our necks for good.

When it comes to those bigger vampires, though, we're obviously going to need a bigger plan, but let's start with our plan for that first group: those minor vampires who steal our peace of mind.

Biting Back: Our Smaller Vampires

Neighbors, coworkers, friends, businesses, lovers, and spouses who refuse to acknowledge our revocations are fairly easy to deal with, and our plan is very simple: We prepare for their next visit by composing a more powerful revocation this time, and this one is going to stick.

Revocations that fail, as we know, do so because the vampire in question doesn't take our will seriously. As far as they're concerned, what we want and what our will is doesn't matter. "Who cares what *you* want?" is what they're really asking by their refusals, and you know what? If they really want to know who cares what we want, then maybe we should tell them. Maybe what somebody else wants—someone more powerful than just we—will get his or her attention and make our point.

Take for instance a coworker whom we've already spoken to about the volume on his radio or his constant interruptions while we're working. When our revocation has failed, when this clown's radio continues to blare and his visits to our cubicle don't stop, then we need to look for more power. At work, we'll find that power sitting—where else? Right in our boss's nice, expensive chair, of course.

We begin by asking our manager or supervisor if we can have a moment of her time, because always remember: timing is important. We must always be mindful of her schedule and when it's convenient for her to listen, or she might not want to help us. She's not going to be in the mood to lend a hand if we're bothering her about it while she's busy: it pays to be patient and it pays to be smart—we strive to be both.

When she indicates she's available, we explain the problem. We tell her about the steps we've already taken to try and solve it ourselves, that they've failed, and that we now feel we need to ask for her help. We see if it would be all right with her if, the next time he bothers us we refer him to her. When this is done correctly, most people—our bosses included—will be happy to help. When she agrees, it's no longer just a matter what our will is, now it's also a matter of what *hers* is, you see? Now we've got more teeth, and sharper ones, at that.

The next time he interrupts us or plays his radio too loudly, we confront him: we start by reminding him of our revocation and point out that he's not complying with it. If he decides at that point that he wants to argue with us about it, we very calmly prevent that by cutting him off (in mid-sentence if necessary), and then referring him to our employer. While our revocation and what *we* wanted clearly mean nothing to him, the chances are he'll find more meaning in what our employer's desires are and what *she* wants.

I have to tell you: there is nothing as effective as a clear statement of our will plus a dash of extra power to get a vampire moving. The same equation would apply to an ex-boy-or-girlfriend who has ignored our will to break it off with them and continues to come to our door, call on our phone, and show up in the most surprising and strangest places (like when when we find ourselves "accidentally" running into them every single day at the store, the post office, a restaurant, or in our rearview mirrors) almost every day since we ended it. Here too, we would handle our next encounter by providing them with a perfect echo of our original revocation, and by pointing out that they are failing to honor the original.

At this stage, we'll want to be prepared because, as you recall, vampires are pretty big fans of engagement. They like to keep the conversation rolling, even if it has to be an argument. Rather than listening to all the good reasons they're going to give us about why their stalking and accidental meetings with us were justified, or getting into a debate about the "rights" they evidently feel they have over our time and our lives—*we stop*. We cut them off, and simply explain that if they do not comply with our request, they can be sure we'll be taking stronger measures to make sure they do from now on.

Here again, clarity about our will alone was not enough to move the vampire back over our threshold, but I'll bet that getting a warning from a cop or a restraining order from the courts will be. I think it's pretty safe to say that when our first revocations are not enough, that: *Clarity of Will + Extra Power = A Much More Effective Revocation*.

Get the process? If someone is hassling you in school, talk to a teacher or principal; if it's a neighbor bothering you, add more family members or housemates to the "power" of your equation. If the trouble is at your local swimming pool or club, talk to security, the director, or administrator there. If it's a telemarketer, ask to speak to their supervisor, and if their supervisor's not there, ask to speak to that supervisor's supervisor, and so on. I've done it, and so can you—and by the way, if someone is bothering you repeatedly at a bar, talk to the bartender, and if that doesn't work, you may need to explain that if they really can't hear you, you can easily call a patrol car and check to see if the police are any more audible to them. Make your revocation clear, and add all the power it takes, one level at a time, until the vampire stops.

Biting Back: Fatal Vampires

If we want to change, we're going to need help—which means that the last place any of us needs to be when we're seeking this new way of life is alone and in the dark. Frankly, we're just begging to be found by some other vampire when we do that, and there's no way around it: we're just going to have to knock that "isolating" crap off. If we're serious about our freedom, we have to get into the light and find other people there who understand exactly what we're going through and can help. And you must believe me when I tell you: these people are everywhere.

So much of what influences the path we'll decide to take depends on the nature of the vampire and our individual experience with it. If we're struggling with drug abuse, we'll want to find drug addicts who are having success in their recovery; if we're struggling with eating disorders, we'll want to find a group of people in a program of recovery that's working for them, and join them. Whatever our troubles have been, we find other people who have struggled with the same things and have not only successfully evicted them, but are also living happily in their success. If we find someone who says they've been free of whatever addiction they had for 30 years but who is clearly miserable, swears all the time, only laughs at mean or horrible things, and doesn't seem to have a lot of friends, well, unless we want to end up like them, we'll probably want to keep looking until we find someone who is both free of the addiction *and* living a good, happy life.

The solution we're seeking should show proof that it works in the people who are using it, and I don't mean to imply that everyone there will be feeling wonderful every minute. Let's be reasonable: they're at meetings or groups for the same reason we are, which of course is that we're unwell and need help. Even so, there should be at least one or two people in the group who have been following their path of recovery and are genuinely happy, peaceful, and free of their addiction—and that's right, you guessed it: those are the people you follow.

When you find members of the group who are living the kind of life you'd like to be living and have the kind of recovery you'd like to have for yourself, then here's what you do:

you ask them how they did it. Ask them to help you, and if it feels right to you, ask them to be your Watcher, too. By joining a group, finding a confidant and mentor to help you find your way, and by following a path that's clearly working for others, not only will you find freedom, but you'll also have living reminders, anytime you want them, of the fact that you are not alone. In time and if you are willing to risk doing what it takes to get it, you will feel a sense of belonging not only in the group, but absolutely everywhere you go.

I'm not kidding.

In my case with alcoholism, which is surely deadliest vampire I've ever fought, I needed to find a new way of living without alcohol. It's one thing to remove a vampire, but it's another to live without it, and since my whole life centered around my vampire—by which I mean the alcohol and drugs—I naturally needed to find new way of living without it. The fact was that I hadn't experienced much living without drugs or alcohol past the age of 15 or so—which meant that by the time I was 36 years old and facing the prospect of living clean and sober, I had to admit and truly believe that I needed help. That's a lot of years to live with an addiction at the hub of your life, and I had a lot of evidence to prove I needed help by the time I stopped. I didn't doubt it. As the titular character of *Jane Eyre* so aptly said, I'd have had to have been "strangely incredulous if I *did* doubt it."

That's the way it is with these really toxic vampires, though: if we lived with them for a very long time, no matter how awful they were, the notion of learning to live without them is still pretty frightening. If we're very blessed, though, at a certain point the prospect of continuing to live the vampire is even more frightening than the prospect of having to learn to live without it. And that's our moment. That is our sacred moment: the one that, if we're willing to receive the gift of clarity if offers, we start running like heck for help.

We know in our hearts where we need to go for that help: if we're being abused, we know to seek a shelter for victims of domestic abuse, a counselor, or official who will take us to where we can get the help we need; if we want to quit smoking and can't, we know to see a doctor who will help us; if we want to put an end to the slavery of our addictions, we know to find specialists or groups that have experience and success with overcoming our addiction, and so on. And then there's one more thing.

I believe that sometimes, if the community or group that offers to help us is one that we've sworn we would *never* go to no matter how awful our lives became; if it is a system, organization, person, or authority that we've always disliked or rejected, then—as strange as it may sound—that might be exactly the place, system, person, or community that's got our name written all over it, by which I mean that it could be the one we most need. Not always, certainly, but sometimes, yes: it really does seem to work that way. For some reason I cannot understand, this resistance we have can be a great divining rod, pointing straight to where we least want, and most need, to go.

Commitment

Commitment is much simpler than you might imagine, and if you think I'm going to tell you now that you have to make a promise, signed in blood, that you will never, ever let your vampire in again, you're wrong. That's not how it works.

Commitment is a thing we do one day—even one moment—at a time, and if you want to know whether or not you're committed to this path to freedom you've chosen, then there is only one question you need ask yourself: "Do I want to stay on this path today—just for today?" If the answer is yes, then that's all you need to know. You've made a promise for today, and it's enough. Exactly enough.

Let's say, though, that you don't feel committed but you truly wish you did. Let's say you want to be committed to leaving a dangerous relationship you're in, but you're too afraid. There's a simple cure for that: you ask the God of your understanding to give you the strength to help you to be willing when the time is right—then just keep asking until the willingness comes. You'll know when it does, and there's just one more thing I'd better warn you about: Look out, because *this works*. When it comes to prayers for willingness, you can always count on getting what you ask for.

Now, what if we are willing and feel committed for that day to what we are doing: let's say we've left an abusive relationship, and it's been going along pretty well for the past two weeks, but then suddenly, in one moment, we find ourselves in a panic? Suddenly we're not sure that we're doing the right thing, and our fears and doubts come pouring in: What were we thinking when we left? How did we ever get talked into this new life? How did we ever get this far from home? What were we—nuts? Is it too late to go back? What should we do?

When every doubt and fear we've ever had comes screaming at us without warning and we are no longer sure we feel committed, here's what we do: We close our eyes and remember exactly what it would be like to be back home with our abuser. We imagine just how it would feel to be there with them right this second. We see and smell the house; we remember every detail, and imagine what we would be doing if we were there at that very moment. When we can see the picture and feel the feeling, then we open our eyes. We look around at where we're sitting right now, and when we've got our bearings, we ask ourselves this one simple question: "If I could be there, back with my abuser, right this second, would I want to be? Or would I, just for this moment, rather be here?"

If our answer is that we'd rather be where we are now, we're as committed as we need to be: this is one day and often one moment at a time, and we mustn't worry about where we think we might want to be tomorrow. Tomorrow will take care of itself. And that's a promise.

Power

We've talked already about some of the kinds of power we have at our disposal, but now it's time to tell you how I really see those powers. From my point of view, all the help that shows up in our lives—the friends, the counselors, the strangers who smile at us for no reason when we most need it, the sunshine that brightens our mood, the knowledge that others are willing to share with us—all of this and more is simply love. When you get right down to it, that love is the real vampire slayer. It is the light and the truth, the compassion and the integrity that no vampire can bear to live in the presence of. And that's why we seek those things: because they are all the "piece" or "peace" as they say, "of God."

I said earlier that there is something inside us that makes us move—and that's power. I also said that there was something else inside that tells us to move this way rather than that, which is guidance. And I'll tell you now: I believe that both of those things are love—they are God, as I understand God, which *is* Love. And Truth. And Justice—in fact, God is all of those things we talked about when we talked about our quest for freedom. There is no doubt in my heart that the power we receive when we ask for help is love, and that if we follow where love takes us in this life, we'll get exactly where we need to go.

Ask the Slayer

First My Brother, Now Me

Slayer,

All my life I've tried to help my brother with his vampires: his depression and negative self-talk. Now it seems the vampire has gotten hold of me—the vampire being my need to rescue my brother. Can you help?

Signed
Worried in the Woods

Dearest Worried,

This may sound hard, but we can't make other people well by getting sick ourselves, and trying to pry the vampire off someone else's neck is sure to do just that: make us sick. This vampire has plenty of appetite for both of you, and can take on you and the rest of your family if you don't get off the menu quick.

One of my favorite principles of practical vampire slaying is:

"If I didn't extend the invitation, then it is not mine to revoke."

As a recovering alcoholic, I can tell you that no one else could make the decision for me to get well. That was my vampire, and my decision. And as you say, this is your vampire now, and your decision to make.

I feel you should find people who have experience with your problem and have gotten free of it. Participation in 12-step groups is great for that, but not the *only* way. They work for me, and I do believe the experienced teacher is best: theory and speculation doesn't cut it with vampires. Look for real power—like the kind we find in the experience and love of others.

PVS

....

III

Living in the Light

11

Spiritual Garlic

Some Thoughts on Gratitude and One of My Favorite Stories About God

EVERY NOW AND THEN I GET A chance to notice how I'm not the same person I used to be. Thank God.

A couple of days ago I was driving home alone from the store with a week or two's worth of groceries piled into the back of the car and imagining what it was going to be like when I got home and started trying to haul all that stuff into the kitchen... and how no one would come to help me.

At first I did the usual: I indulged in a masochistic daydream of how my daughter, her friend who was visiting, and my husband would all have their shoes off and be doing lazy things when I walked in hauling all those groceries—and how they would therefore be oblivious to my struggles. So I started to get mad about this thing that wasn't real and hadn't even happened yet. Then years of slayer training stopped me.

I reached into my coat pocket, pulled out my cell phone, and called home. When my daughter answered, I told her I was planning to be home in about five minutes and asked her if she, her friend, and her dad wouldn't mind putting their shoes on so they could help me bring all those bags inside.

That was fine with her.

When I drove up, they came out and helped me bring everything in. In fact, I stayed inside and started putting things away while they finished, and when we were done and I'd given my daughter and her friend some lunch (a treat I'd brought them from Subway™), I asked them which they wanted to do when they were through eating: to take our little cairn terrier, Agatha, out for a walk, or to give her a bath. I said that whichever one they didn't want to do, I would.

So about an hour later I gave Agatha, a nice warm bath—but *first* I got to do what I wanted, which was to write. Instead of spending the rest of my day mad because everyone had ignored me when I came in with the groceries and they hadn't been able to read my mind, I was enjoying myself, writing, and no one else was worried or confused or upset or trying to figure out why I was acting so nasty since I'd come back from the store, because I *wasn't* confusing anyone, and I *wasn't* acting nasty.

I want to tell you, there's a lot of freedom in that for me. The reason it came to me that there was another way to handle that situation is that I've been practicing these slayer principles for a while now, and most of the time I'd rather feel happy and free than miserable and right. Little by little and with practice, this has slowly become a part of who I am and a way of life for me—probably because I *like* feeling good instead of bad, and sticking to this plan I've learned about how to handle my vampires works so well that I actually remember to do it most of the time. It's a Pavlovian thing.

It's nice, this living in the light, and it's got me thinking about the things I do to keep myself there as much as possible so I can share them with you. I know what the first and most important thing I do is: It's to keep asking for help from my friends, Watchers, and community, and to make sure I'm available to give help back to them when they need it, too.

Sharing our vampire slaying stories, both the victorious and the not so victorious, is one of the most powerful ways to stay in the light that I know of. When I remember to ask my friends or Watchers for help, I get a chance to hear my story out loud, and by having to make it clear to somebody else what's going on with me, I make it clear to myself. Once I've found that clarity, I can either do something about it or just accept it and let it go. Even when I know all the rules, even when I'm willing to take responsibility for my invitations and even when I know *everything* there is to know about vampires and vampire slaying, life can still kick my butt so hard sometimes I can hardly get out of bed. In fact, sometimes I'm lucky if I can get as far as the telephone or my computer and then call or write a friend for help, if you want to call that luck. You might want to call it grace—or I might.

But talk about the rules: there's one for you. No matter how well equipped I may think I am, there's no way I'm going to keep going without the love and help of my friends. Learning the rules and trying to practice them helps immensely, but it's not nearly enough if we isolate—neither giving nor receiving help. When we hear from friends who are having a bad time with their own vampires, we have an opportunity to search our memories for what worked for us in their situation, and to offer them love and support, too. And we all know who benefits most from helping: it's always the helper. We just can't lose.

So that's another way to stay in the light: by sharing experience and trying to be there for our friends and fellow slayers.

About God

When I was a kid, no one ever taught me how to find a God that was personal to me. I went to church here and there for a few years, but no one ever suggested that a relationship with God was like any other relationship I might want to have: that I had to start sharing myself with that person and listening for their responses if I wanted to know them better. That was something I had to learn how to do from friends and Watchers and by just plain doing it myself. I had to start my relationship with a God I didn't know anything about the same way I did with anyone else: I had to strike up a conversation and see what God had to say.

Did I ever tell you what the first Watcher I ever had—the Amazing Catherine—told me I should try to do if I wanted to get well from alcoholism? She said that I should—every single morning and no matter what—ask a God I had absolutely no conception of to help me stay clean and sober for that day.

She recommended that I say, "Please keep me clean and sober today," every morning and then I was supposed to thank this God I didn't even know for keeping me sober at the end of every day, too. She said she didn't care that I didn't know who or what I was praying to, and she didn't care whether I believed it or not—said it wasn't important. She said to just do it, and because I was a little short on good ideas of my own in those days, I went ahead and followed her directions.

What I didn't know back then was how, in doing that one little thing, I was initiating a relationship with a God I didn't know. It was just like in the 6th grade when there was a new girl in school I wanted to know better: I started talking with her to see what she'd say and how she'd act. It was a very practical piece of advice Catherine gave me, because what she really supplied me with was an opening line: a question I could ask so I could get to know God better. The question she'd given me was, "Would you please help to keep me sober today?" and over time I realized God's response was, "You bet." It must have been, because I stayed clean and sober.

That was a lot of information to gather about this character. It told me a lot about the nature of God and the power of love, about how closely God listens, no matter what I believe or don't believe—and one other thing: it taught me how ready and waiting this God was for me to start talking.

Right now.

Spiritual Garlic

Everyone knows about garlic and vampires. It reminds me of some old household cure that's been handed down for generations or something, like chicken soup for colds. I bet you could even call your mom right now and ask her what to take for a vampire, and she'd say, "Garlic. Lots of garlic."

So what's the story with garlic anyway? Old Father Callahan in Stephen King's *'Salem's Lot* suggests it might be an allergy vampires have to it, and I certainly like the sound of that. It's something we can all relate to, anyway. Most of us have experience with allergies or things that we feel a definite need to stay away from, like me with mildewed towels or those home crafting projects people do. Everyone's got something that gives them the shivers—but when it comes to vampires and garlic, the effect seems to be unusually strong.

There's a clue to solving this mystery about vampires and garlic at our local health food stores. That's where I found my first clue, anyway—on the label of a garlic supplement there. Among the many other benefits this fabulous product has to offer us, there is this:

"Garlic has long been known to be
an excellent blood purifier."

That's the one we're interested in, right there: that *garlic purifies the blood.*

Now, just hang on to that thought, please—and then juxtapose it with this one: There is a scene in *'Salem's Lot* where the master vampire, Barlow, is shooting the breeze before dinner with his next victim. Barlow has an enormous ego and is kind of a blabbermouth besides, and he seems to be hypnotizing this guy before he sinks his fangs into him so he can get the "o.k." before he does, don't you know (there's always an invitation first—*always*).

Barlow is going on about how much he's enjoying his stay in *'Salem's Lot*, and he starts to get so carried away with himself that pretty soon he's even explaining to this poor guy about what it is in the residents' blood he loves so dearly. Here's what he says—and I'm paraphrasing, I hope more or less correctly:

"... their blood is filled with the of the kind of hatred and
darkness so essential to the strength of the vampire."

So it is this "hatred and darkness" in the blood of the vampire's victims that accounts for this extraordinary ability it has to... refresh: to satisfy and delight the vampire. Isn't that just *fun*?

It reminds me of when I was living in Alaska and it was time (as local vernacular had it) to "get a moose," because that's when

I found out that the flavor of the meat depended a lot on what the animal had eaten. If pickings were slim that year and the moose was forced to live on needles and branches, the meat wasn't expected to taste very good. The relationship between what it ate and how good it tasted had never occurred to me at all before I learned that—but now, of course, it makes perfect sense. And I'm sure you can see where I'm going with this, because how did that go again? That garlic is a blood *purifier*?

Maybe in the same way that you and I don't care for the taste of the meat on an animal that's been eating poorly, our vampires don't care for the taste of blood that is purified by garlic. Maybe if our blood is pure it can even gag them, so they go, "Ptui! Ack! I can't eat *this*!"

So I was thinking: what if we, as slayers, could "purify" our own "blood"? That would be useful, don't you think? Wouldn't it be cool, to say nothing of practical, if we could provoke a sort of allergic reaction in our practical vampires?

The question, though, is how to do it. How can we purify our own blood of the hatred and darkness that Barlow speaks of? And I know the answer: it's confession.

I'm not suggesting we all go running off to church, but I am suggesting the use of something I call "spiritual garlic"—a practice of prayer and meditation that leave us clean and purified at the end of every day.

I think I should start by saying that if this looks familiar to any members of 12-step groups or religious bodies, it certainly should. I don't make these rules and principles up by myself, you know—they're true and they work because they've always been true and they've always worked. That's what a principle *is*: something that's true; always has been and always will be.

Before we go to bed at night, we turn everything off so we can concentrate, and then we call on the place inside of us that connects to our God. Then we start to remember our day—almost as if we were watching a movie of it: We watch what we did, and as we do, we ask ourselves these questions:

- Where was I selfish today?
- Where was I scared?
- How could I have handled that situation (at work, at home, with friends, at the store, wherever) that upset me or someone else in a better way, and how can I do it differently next time?
- Did I hurt anyone today? Do I need to make amends?
- Did I forget anything that I meant to do and need to remember for tomorrow?
- And most importantly: *is there anything I've kept to myself that I need to share with another person right away?* Is there anything I've pushed into the dark that needs to come into the light?
- Have I put anything out of balance that needs to be corrected?

As we see these things, we ask for God's help with them. We ask what we need to do to correct any mistakes we've made, and we ask God to give us an answer about how we can handle each situation better next time. Because the purifier, or garlic, is the act of self-assessment, and the power behind it is God's love and help.

And not a vampire in the world can be exposed to that much pure light and hope to survive.

As we're watching our "movie" we may get sidetracked: we may begin to see all the wonderful things that happened in our day and the things that made us happy: maybe it's a laugh we shared with someone or a new friend we've made, or maybe it's a recipe we've never tried before that everybody loved. It might be something our spouse did that surprised us. It could be how fast our children are growing or how blessed we feel to have friends: whatever it is, we say, "thank you." We ask God to help us be the person God would have us be, and ask for God's tender mercies for our brothers and sisters everywhere. Then we say, "thank you," again, and go to sleep, knowing there is no lingering hatred in our "blood," and that we're current, present, and thus with God.

The God you speak to is your own and the word choice is of course up to you, but the idea behind this is to clean up at the end of the day: to make peace with God and yourself, so tomorrow you can start fresh, and stay in the present.

And I have to say that it works like crazy, pretty much.

Practical Gratitude

Here is one of the best stories I've ever heard about God. God is a guy in this story and heaven is in the sky, I guess—and as silly as that may sound, it's the way I first heard it, and so I like it this way. It goes like this:

God walks into his office one morning and says to his assistant, "So what have we got going so far today?" and the assistant checks his notepad and says, "Well... so far this morning we've got about 200 million guys asking for money and about 45 thousand teenagers who want you to fix it so they don't get caught skipping school. There's another 75 million asking you to get even with their bosses for them and about 200 million more in their cars on their way to work, begging you to teach the guys ahead of them how to drive."

"Uh huh," God says, unwrapping and popping a piece of butterscotch into his mouth, "and that's it?"

And the assistant says, "Well, no, actually, there's this one other guy down there, too. He's on his knees praying, and he just keeps saying, 'Thank you, thank you, thank you, thank you' over and over again."

And God says, "Give him anything he wants."

....

One time, early in my recovery when I was first learning how to stick around outside and talk to people after meetings, another member of my 12-step group came up to me and said something nice to me about the way I looked.

Well. I of course did what I always did in those days: I immediately launched into an argument with him about why he was wrong to compliment me. I pulled the old deflection routine. I said, "Oh. Well that's because I finally got a little *sleep* last night," or, "Yeah, I know what you mean: this sweater I'm wearing is so beautiful it's impossible to *not* look good in it," or, "What are you—in a good mood or something?"

I won't torture you with more examples, because I think you might already have a pretty good idea of what I'm talking about. So many of us do it: that thing where we throw a compliment right back in someone's face before it has a chance to reach us.

Once again, however, there was another Watcher of mine on the scene: this time it was one of my best friends, Dave, and what he did was—he sort of leaned over to me, balancing on one leg, and then out of the side of his mouth, whispered, "Just say 'thank you.'"

It shook me up there for a second, and I almost started telling Dave why *he* was wrong, too, but by that time I was becoming sort of "automatically obedient" to my Watchers, and so I just looked at the guy, laughed, and said, "Thank you."

Dave never explained to me why he had corrected me or what he meant by that, but I started to practice that way of responding to people more often anyway, and this funny thing started happening to me: I started feeling better after I got a compliment.

It was almost like, if somebody told me I looked good and I said "thank you" instead of pushing the remark away, then it started to sort of *enter* me, I guess. I finally started to understand that, at least for me, I couldn't receive what I wouldn't say thank you for, and all those years of pushing away the love and kindness that was being offered to me had left me absolutely starving for it.

How obvious that seems to me now: that I cannot receive what I will not say "thank you" for, and when I keep refusing love is when I always end up feeling unloved and wondering why I feel that way.

Some days I feel like I have ask God to help me receive what's being offered to me that day, just as it is, because I know I won't do it without God's help—I'll mess it up with some strange idea I have about looking humble or thinking I'm unworthy of what's being offered. That's one thing I love about the "thank you" guy in the story: he's not missing even one tiny little bit of what's being offered to him because he's always being thankful for it—like he just assumes there's always something to be grateful for. But there's one other thing I love about that story, too.

I hesitate to tell you, because when I first heard the story about God in the office no one told *me* how to think about it: my personal understanding of what it meant to me just sort of evolved, and I'd really like for that to happen for you, too, but I have to tell you anyway, just because I do.

I love that God's answer to the assistant is: "Give him anything he wants," and it's not because I believe God is rewarding him for his gratitude, either. Although I think it could easily be misinterpreted to mean that.

What I think instead is this: when God says, "give him anything he wants" it's because when we say "thank you" to everything, then everything we *receive* automatically morphs into everything we *want*. I believe gratitude has the power to do that: to change the things that we didn't know we wanted into the things we do want—everything we want, in fact.

Remember how I was telling you my Watcher Catherine not only wanted me to ask God to keep me clean and sober at the beginning of every day—but also wanted me to say "thank you for keeping me clean and sober" at the end of every day, too?

I can tell you that at the time I really wasn't so sure that being sober was what I wanted, and that I wasn't so sure I felt the gratitude I was expressing at night for it, either. But I am now.

And I swear to you, for what it's worth, every time I say "thank you," God looks down at me from that office and says, "Give her anything she wants." It sure feels like that's what I've been getting for a long time now: that, and a whole lot more.

So if you've got a vampire hanging around and it's stealing your gifts of life and free will, you can bite back if you need to—and in fact, it's really only right that you do. Remember, though, while you're doing it, to be neither ashamed nor proud.

Oh—and for heaven's sake, don't forget to say, "thank you."

Acknowledgments

IF ONE OF THE MOST INSPIRING WOMEN I've ever known, Jennifer Graf Groneberg, hadn't shown me how to do this and given me unaccountably generous and thoughtful gifts of her precious time and advice, those gorgeous earrings, delicious soups, and her practical, Watcherly love—there would be no book, and that's for sure. You've taught me so many things I never knew about what real friends do and how good people really behave. Thank you, Jennifer.

If my sister, Julia Nowicki, hadn't jumped on board with her instant enthusiasm and trust, her amazing ability to make things happen, the many trips to Chicago and gifts of simply everything she gave me that helped make me feel like a real writer, and if not for her every-single-day-never-faltering confidence that I was going to finish it, this book simply would not be here. Thank you, Julia.

If not for the careful listening, continuous support, and life-saving wisdom of my Mom and Dad, of my wonderful, encouraging brother Mike and my discerning, truly funny and deeply loving sister Joan, of my beloved Robert, my darling Madeline Jane, and our sweet little Agatha—forget about it. I could not have done this. Thank you for believing in me. There are no words for how much I love you.

If not for the tender care, excellent chauffeur service, and best pizza I've ever eaten that Judith Bromley gave me, and if not for her incredible talent besides, I'd not have had the energy in the summer of '08 to work, and worse—there'd be no pictures! Thank you, Judith, for so much.

If Julie Wenner, one night so long ago at dinner, hadn't dared me to write a letter to Stephen King and then continued to cheer me on forever; if Milana Marsenich hadn't given me two days of her life to type and format my chapters when I was flat out of time; and if I'd had to live without the incomprehensibly enduring support of Janice Doble, Angela Nolan, Mary Gertson, Jan Myers, Chrisse Harnos, Anthony Lucero, Sharla Roberts, Sherri Cornelius, Sarah Smith, Jane Levy, Suzanne Kincaid, Phyllis Walker, Cindy Doll, Gary Acevedo, Jo Anne Hines, every member of the Wild Horse Writer's Group, all the employees of the Polson City Library and more people in town than I can count, I don't see how this book could have been born, either. Thank you, my wonderful friends.

I have to say, too, that if hadn't been for those early days at the CSKT Division of Lands and the hilarious, sincere contributions made by my dear friends George DuCharme, Marla Couture, and M'Lissa McElderry—and if not for the help and encouragement of Li Erickson, Beth Hutchings, and Lori Lasche way back when, too—I might never have thought it was worth trying to write this. Thanks, guys.

If Stephen King hadn't written *'Salem's Lot*, which soothed and inspired me for years, and if there were no 12-step programs, which have also soothed and inspired me for years, again: there'd be no book. Thanks, Mr. King. Thanks, 12-step groups.

To Dr. Loren Rourke, Dr. Paul Gochis, Dr. Michael Goodman, Dr. Gordon Stille, Dr. Katie Carter, and countless, angelically kind, skillful, and patient nurses and aides: thank you all for my life.

To three extraordinarily brilliant and generous women with hearts of gold: Joan Walsh, Jaye Wells, and Melody Beattie. Thank you for your time, support, and most of all, friendship.

And finally, to my dear agent Jacky Sach, to my fabulous editor and new friend, Carrie Obry, to the superlative talent of Laura Graves and the perfectly amazing team at Llewellyn: for your time and expertise, your imagination, confidence, dedication, and on top of all that, your friendship: thank you. You shocked the heck out of me when you taught me what publishing was all about. I had no idea it was so full of love.